To Have and Have Not

Wisconsin/Warner Bros. Screenplay Series

To Have
and Have Not

Edited with an introduction by

Bruce F. Kawin

Published for the Wisconsin Center for Film and Theater Research by
The University of Wisconsin Press

Published 1980

The University of Wisconsin Press
114 North Murray Street
Madison, Wisconsin 53715

The University of Wisconsin Press, Ltd.
1 Gower Street
London WC1E HA, England

First printing

Printed in the United States of America

For LC CIP information see the colophon

ISBN 0-299-08090-0 cloth; 0-299-08094-3 paper

Publication of this volume has been assisted by a grant from
The Brittingham Fund, Inc.

Contents

Foreword

In donating the Warner Film Library to the Wisconsin Center for Film and Theater Research in 1969, along with the RKO and Monogram film libraries and UA corporate records, United Artists created a truly great resource for the study of American film. Acquired by United Artists in 1957, during the period when the major studios sold off their films for use on television, the Warner library is by far the richest portion of the gift, containing eight hundred sound features, fifteen hundred short subjects, nineteen thousand still negatives, legal files, and press books, in addition to screenplays for the bulk of the Warner Brothers product from 1930 to 1950. For the purposes of this project, the company has granted the Center whatever publication rights it holds to the Warner films. In so doing, UA has provided the Center another opportunity to advance the cause of film scholarship.

Our goal in publishing these screenplays is to explicate the art of screenwriting during the thirties and forties, the so-called Golden Age of Hollywood. In preparing a critical introduction and annotating the screenplay, the editor of each volume is asked to cover such topics as the development of the screenplay from its source to the final shooting script, differences between the final shooting script and the release print, production information, exploitation and critical reception of the film, its historical importance, its directorial style, and its position within the genre. He is also encouraged to go beyond these guidelines to incorporate supplemental information concerning the studio system of motion picture production.

We could set such an ambitious goal because of the richness of the script files in the Warner Film Library. For many film titles, the files might contain the property (novel, play, short story, or original story idea), research materials, variant drafts and scripts (from story outline to treatment to shooting script), post-production items such as press books and dialogue continuities, and legal records (details of the acquisition of the property, copyright registration, and contracts with actors and directors). Editors of the Wisconsin/Warner Bros. Screenplay Series receive copies of all the materials, along with prints of the films (the most authoritative ones available for reference purposes), to use in preparing the introductions and annotating the final shooting scripts.

In the process of preparing the screenplays for publication, typographical errors were corrected, punctuation and capitalization were modernized, and the format was redesigned to facilitate readability.

Unless otherwise specified, the photographs are frame enlargements taken from a 35-mm print of the film provided by United Artists.

In theory, the Center should have received the extant scripts of all pre-1951 Warner Brothers productions when the United Artists Collection was established. Recent events, however, have created at least some doubt in this area. Late in 1977, Warners donated collections consisting of the company's production records and distribution records to the University of Southern California and Princeton University respectively. The precise contents of the collections are not known, since at the present time they are not generally open to scholars. To the best of our knowledge, all extant scripts have been considered in the preparation of these volumes. Should any other versions be discovered at a later date, we will recognize them in future printings of any volumes so affected.

Tino Balio
General Editor

Introduction: *No Man Alone*

Bruce F. Kawin

The story of the making of *To Have and Have Not* is an exciting and complex one, ranging from the well-known romance between its stars, Humphrey Bogart and Lauren Bacall, to one of the subtler developments of the alliance between the U.S. government and the Batista regime in Cuba. It is also the story of a collaboration among four very fine writers: Ernest Hemingway, Howard Hawks, Jules Furthman, and William Faulkner. Although the film builds on the contributions of two Nobel Prize winners, a scenarist of the first rank, a masterful cinematographer, a skillful editor, and such creative actors as Walter Brennan, Marcel Dalio, Hoagy Carmichael, and of course Bogart and Bacall, it is also that auteur critic's dream, a film that clearly reveals the guiding influence and personal vision of a single artist, Howard Hawks, who conceived, produced, rewrote, and directed this tough-edged, sexy, comic melodrama. "I can make a picture out of your worst story," Hawks once told Hemingway. It was not Hemingway's worst story, and Hawks did not make a picture out of it; what he made instead is an entertaining and unpretentious masterpiece.

The Novel

With the exception of *For Whom the Bell Tolls*, *To Have and Have Not* is Hemingway's only deliberate and sustained attempt at political commentary. In part, it was a response to such critics as Wyndham Lewis who had come, in the light of the Depression, to disparage Hemingway's fiction for being "entirely closed to poli-

Introduction

tics."[1] It was also, and more crucially, a response to the conditions Hemingway observed during a layover in Havana in 1933, on the first leg of a trip to Madrid, Paris, and Africa.

Brigadier General Gerardo Machado y Morales had been elected president of Cuba in 1924 and enjoyed great popular support until 1929. The sugar industry prospered, relations with government and banking forces in the United States were mutually satisfactory, and a large public works project improved the roads, the public buildings, the hospitals, and the schools. By 1929, however, Machado had decided to emulate Mussolini. At just the time he was coming to seem like a brutal megalomaniac, the Depression hit Cuba, and it became impossible for Machado to silence his critics by pointing to a solid economy. On September 30, 1930, the Havana police killed a student demonstrator, and from then until 1933, Cuba was in turmoil, mostly in the form of battles between terrorist student groups and the army and police. In July 1933, Machado temporarily restored constitutional rights and found that he had unwittingly sanctioned a public protest against his regime.[2] During the first days of August there was a general strike. Hemingway, who was in Havana between August 4 and 7, privately endorsed the cause of the people and referred to Machado as a "lousy tyrant."[3] The day he sailed for Europe there were false rumors of Machado's resignation; cheering crowds were massacred in the streets. On August 12 Machado fled the country. Within five months Colonel Fulgencio Batista y Zaldívar had taken control.

When Hemingway arrived in Madrid, he found the Spanish Republic in a shaky condition. An inefficient bureaucracy appeared to have absorbed the liberal idealists, and it was Hemingway's guess that another revolution was on the way. He was coming to feel that the process of revolution and the interests of the indi-

1. Carlos Baker, *Hemingway: The Writer as Artist* (Princeton: Princeton University Press, 1963), p. 203.
2. John Edwin Fagg, *Cuba, Haiti, and the Dominican Republic* (Englewood Cliffs, N.J.: Prentice-Hall, 1965), pp. 74–82.
3. Carlos Baker, *Ernest Hemingway: A Life Story* (New York: Scribner's, 1969), p. 245.

vidual were opposed. While in Madrid, in September 1933, he wrote a story that became Part One of *To Have and Have Not;* called "One Trip Across," it celebrated the virtues of a tough, independent fisherman, Harry Morgan, who becomes a smuggler rather than let his family go hungry. When he returned to his Key West home in 1935, Hemingway wrote the second part of the novel, a story called "The Tradesman's Return." In July 1936, he decided to rework these stories into a novel about the nature of revolution and the decline of the individual.[4] At that point the Spanish Civil War broke out, intensely focusing Hemingway's political consciousness.

He wanted to be in Spain but felt he had to finish the novel. The first draft of *To Have and Have Not* was completed in January 1937. Hemingway then went to Spain, where he wrote the voice-over narration for Joris Ivens's film *The Spanish Earth* (1937).[5] Back in America during the late summer, he spent two weeks revising the proof sheets of the novel, which was as close as he got to doing a second draft.

To Have and Have Not was published by Scribner's in October 1937 and became a best-seller. The critics tended generally not to like it; although they patted Hemingway on the back for showing "social consciousness," many considered the book structurally flawed, confused, preachy, and even sloppy. In his typical fashion Hemingway—who was never able to accept criticism gracefully—assumed that the critics had ganged up on him and became bitter about the whole matter.[6] His rejecting attitude, his angry and self-pitying isolationism, is ironically appropriate, since the basic theme of the novel is that one man alone has no chance against large, hostile forces. I say "ironically" since it is just this theme that Hawks, Furthman, and Faulkner reversed, and it is

4. Baker, *Hemingway,* pp. 203–204.

5. This commentary was first recorded by Orson Welles, but Ivens soon substituted Hemingway's own reading of the text. Apparently both versions are now in circulation.

6. Baker, *Ernest Hemingway,* pp. 320–21. Compare Hemingway's response to the critics of *Across the River and into the Trees,* who were later cast as the sharks in *The Old Man and the Sea.*

their celebration of the *power* of the individual and the momentum of the anti-Fascist cause that has accounted for much of the film's success. In emphasizing what he saw as the positive elements of Hemingway's vision, Hawks also rejected that current of self-pity (or perhaps it should be called an embattled defeatism) that wears down many of the novel's characters and that was a consistent feature of Hemingway's imagination and of his personal life.

Hemingway, Furthman, Faulkner, and Hawks all had different versions of Harry Morgan, and it is interesting to observe how well Humphrey Bogart could have played any of them. Furthman's was a tough adventurer, Faulkner's a sometime misogynist on the verge of political commitment, and Hawks's a witty and self-confident professional—but Hemingway's was a family man, an ex-cop, a desperate planner, an unsentimental killer, an individualist ground to death by giant forces, a loser.

The novel opens in a bar in Havana, where Morgan refuses to carry three Cuban terrorists to the States and then watches them get shot up in the streets. He goes to his charter-fishing boat and meets his friend Eddy, a rummy who "used to be a good man." They take the client, Mr. Johnson, out for a day of fishing; Johnson hooks two huge fish and loses them both, along with Morgan's expensive rod and reel. Johnson says he'll pay Morgan the next day, but instead flies to Florida. Unable to pay for new equipment, and needing money to support his wife, Marie, and their three daughters (who live in Key West), Morgan agrees to smuggle some Chinese out of Cuba. The man who hires him, Mr. Sing, clearly expects him to drown the cargo. On his way to pick up the Chinese, Morgan discovers that Eddy has stowed away on the boat and decides he will have to kill him. After loading the men, Morgan strangles Mr. Sing, puts the furious cargo more or less ashore, and heads home to Key West, having decided not to kill Eddy after all.

The second part of the novel finds Morgan smuggling liquor from Cuba to Florida. It is about six months later, and the implication is that he was never able to finance a return to the charter-fishing business. He is in his boat with a Negro named Wesley, and both have been shot—Wesley in the leg and Morgan in the arm. They are spotted again, and Morgan dumps the liquor overboard. The third and longest part of the novel is set a few months later in Key West. Morgan's boat has been impounded (thanks to the man who spotted him) and his arm has been amputated. Robert Simmons, a lawyer Morgan refers to as Bee-lips, hires him to take four Cubans to Havana after they rob a bank (to finance the anti-Machado terrorists). Morgan hires Albert Tracy, a workman on relief, to be his mate. After an unsuccessful attempt to steal back his own boat, Morgan gets Simmons to rent the boat belonging to Freddy, the proprietor of the bar where much of the action of this part of the novel takes place. Then he spends the night with Marie.[7]

At this point Hemingway introduces a whole new set of characters: rich writers and businessmen who hang around Freddy's bar or loll in their yachts. The central figure is Richard Gordon, a writer apparently based in part on John Dos Passos, who is trying to write a proletarian novel and who is both conceited and insensitive. While his long-suffering wife, Helen, explores her friendship with a Professor MacWalsey, Gordon goes to bed with a rich bitch named Helène Bradley, who "collected writers as well as their books." When Gordon gets home, he and Helen have a brilliantly written fight and realize their marriage is over. Back at Freddy's, Gordon gets drunk with a large group of workers on relief,[8] picks a fight with MacWalsey, gets knocked out by the bouncer, and stumbles home.

7. Marie is forty-five (two years Morgan's senior), a bleached blonde with an extensive sexual past. She might be described as a Molly Bloom metamorphosed by suffering and compassion.

8. These workers are based on a real community that was wiped out in a 1935 hurricane. Hemingway helped collect the two hundred bodies and wrote about that experience for *New Masses*. One of Morgan's central compulsions is not to go on welfare. Hemingway's reference to these workers, and Albert's fate in the novel, help show the reader why Morgan's tragic position makes sense.

The story of the Gordons is told in parallel with that of Morgan's final voyage.[9] This parallel montage is the source of most critics' objections to the novel.

Morgan prepares Freddy's boat, the *Queen Conch*, for the voyage, hiding a gun near the engine. The bank is robbed, and one of the terrorists (Roberto) kills Simmons. The four Cubans pile aboard, and Roberto horribly and suddenly kills Albert. Morgan buys time by setting a course that will miss Cuba, engages in a discussion of revolutionary tactics and priorities with the youngest of the radicals, and decides to himself that no one with real sympathy for the working man could have killed Albert. Late that night he kills all four of them with the hidden gun, but is mortally gut-shot in the process. The boat drifts till late the next day, when it is found by the Coast Guard. Before losing consciousness, Morgan tells the men who have found him, "No matter how a man alone ain't got no bloody fucking chance."[10] Hemingway felt this was the message of his book[11] and observes in the narrative that this is what it had taken Morgan his whole life to learn. As the boat is towed into the harbor, Hemingway surveys the bedrooms of the various yachts and with them the failures of the upper classes; it is a bitter chapter. Morgan dies in the hospital without regaining consciousness, and Marie prepares herself for a life without meaning, hoping that it will be easier if she dies inside. The last sentence of the novel describes a yacht "hugging the reef as she made to the westward to keep from wasting fuel against the stream."

9. One of the intersections of these plots, chapter 19, is a high point of the novel. The day before his affair with Helène, Gordon passes Marie on the street; she is returning from the sheriff's office, presumably having reported Morgan missing. Gordon is convinced he understands her—her ugliness, her sexual unresponsiveness, her lack of sympathy for her husband, and a number of other qualities he invents—and rushes home to write a chapter about her. Toward the end of the novel Marie drives past Gordon as he heads home after his fight in the bar and dismisses him as a poor rummy. She is, of course, a better judge of character than he is.

10. Ernest Hemingway, *To Have and Have Not* (New York: Scribner's, 1937), p. 225.

11. Baker, *Ernest Hemingway*, p. 383.

Wasting fuel against the stream is what most of the people in this novel have been doing, and the stream is not just an image of malevolent Fate but also one of the Depression (and the government's manner of handling it). A man alone has little chance against such forces, and even men banded together for revolution are presented as having lost sight of their goals. (The only exception appears to be a radical Gordon meets in the bar, who tells him his books are "shit.") The solo artist, at least one like Gordon, has fewer moral resources and less real success even than Morgan, who at least never quits. This is the key to the novel's title, which refers to two sets of haves and have-nots: those with or without life and money, and those with or without guts and moral power. The function of the parallel plotting in Part Three of the novel is to orchestrate these social, economic, and psychological disparities; no solution is suggested.

The points of contact between this novel and the film that uses its name are slight. Walter Brennan's Eddy is related to the novel's rummy Eddy and also to Albert Tracy. The fishing scene with Johnson is hardly changed, and in both stories Morgan's financial hardship leads to his having to deal with radicals. The Gordons undergo several metamorphoses until Helen and Helène show up as Helene de Bursac and Gordon is lost in the shuffle. Wesley becomes Horatio, and the *Queen Conch* keeps her name but changes ownership. And that's about it.

Fishing for a Writer

So one day Ernest Hemingway and Howard Hawks went off on a ten-day fishing trip.

Hawks had been trying to get Hemingway to write scripts for some time, but Hemingway had said he was good at what he was already doing and didn't want to go to Hollywood. "You don't have to go to Hollywood." said Hawks. "We can meet just the way we're doing now. You don't even have to write down the story—I'll dictate it." Hemingway remained adamant, and Hawks said, "Ernest, you're a damn fool. You need money, you know. You can't do all the things you'd like to do. If I make three dollars in a picture, you get one of them. I can make a picture out of your worst story."[12] "What's my worst story?" asked Hemingway. "That god damned bunch of junk called *To Have and To Have Not* [sic]." "You can't make anything out of that," said Hemingway, and Hawks said, "Yes I can. You've got the character of Harry Morgan; I think I can give you the wife. All you have to do is make a story about how they met."

They planned a story during the next several days, on Hemingway's boat; all this probably occurred early in 1939. In May 1939, Hemingway sold all movie, radio, and TV rights in his novel to the Hughes Tool Co. (with which Hawks had connections) for $10,000. In October 1943, Hawks bought these rights from Hughes for $92,500 and sold them to Warner Brothers for $92,500 plus a quarter interest in the picture. "When I told [Hemingway] how much that picture made," Hawks later said, "and I said, 'You only got $10,000,' he wouldn't talk to me for six months."

Hawks was a great teaser, and one of the things he told Hemingway in a last-ditch attempt to get him to write this script probably struck a nerve. "Okay," he said, "I'll get Faulkner to do it; he can write better than you can anyway." (The story may, of course, have been invented years later, long after the events of 1944 had in fact brought Faulker onto the picture.)[13] Hemingway is on record as having admitted twice—to James T. Farrell in 1936 and to Jean-Paul Sartre in 1944—that Faulkner was a better writer than he, but he could hardly have enjoyed anyone else's pointing this out. In 1947, when Faulkner made his statement that the best

12. Much of this information and all Hawks quotations come from an unpublished interview between Hawks and myself on May 24, 1976. For further background on Hawks and Faulkner, see Bruce Kawin, *Faulkner and Film* (New York: Ungar, 1977) and Meta Carpenter Wilde and Orin Borsten, *A Loving Gentleman* (New York: Simon and Schuster, 1976).

13. Hawks's stories were often unreliable. One has to distrust especially those stories that contain ironic coincidences—a completely unfounded one, for instance, of Faulkner's working in a bookstore and selling *The Sound and the Fury* to unsuspecting customers. Lauren Bacall says this of her own first experiences with Hawks's stories: "He took me to lunch and told me about his directing experiences with various actresses. It was always what he said to them, or to Howard Hughes, to Jack Warner—he always came out on top, he always won. He was mesmerizing and I believed every story he told me." (Lauren Bacall, *Lauren Bacall by Myself* [New York: Knopf, 1979], p. 79.)

Introduction

modern novelists were Wolfe, Dos Passos, Caldwell, Hemingway, and himself, and that of the five Wolfe had the most experimental courage and Hemingway the least, Hemingway was furious; feeling his courage in general had been maligned, he got a friend to write Faulkner about his war record! Faulkner apologized, but that apparently didn't do much good.

When in 1952 Faulkner praised Hemingway's independence as a writer, Hemingway decided he had been insulted again; he apparently never saw a review Faulkner wrote shortly thereafter, to the effect that *The Old Man and the Sea* was perhaps "the best single piece of any of us—I mean his and my contemporaries." By 1955 Hemingway was referring to Faulkner as "Old Corndrinking Mellifluous," and by 1956 as "a no-good son of a bitch."[14] Although Hawks continually urged Faulkner and Hemingway to meet, they always refused—something Hawks considered amusing.

Faulkner's attitudes toward Hemingway were less motivated by egotism. In 1955 he explained his "courage" ranking as follows: "I rated Wolfe first, myself second. I put Hemingway last. I said we were all failures. All of us had failed to match the dream of perfection and I rated the authors on the basis of their splendid failure to do the impossible. . . . I rated Hemingway last because he stayed with what he knew. He did it fine, but he didn't try for the impossible."[15] There is no record of his judgment on *To Have and Have Not*, but in his 1942 original screenplay, "The De Gaulle Story" (Warner Brothers, unproduced), he had one of his characters praise *For Whom the Bell Tolls* as a source of political and personal inspiration:

EMILIE: But after we reached Paris, and they overtook us again, and it was no use to flee again, because now nothing remained that we could be despoiled of, another musician, a Frenchman, a young man who knew Father, would come to see us. And one night he brought a book, an American book written by a Mr. Hemingway. He would read it to us at night and translate it. It told about a young girl to whom that [i.e., rape by soldiers] had happened also, and about an older woman who was very

14. Baker, *Ernest Hemingway*, pp. 297, 439, 461, 503–504, 532, 534.
15. Harvey Breit, "A Walk with Faulkner," *New York Times Book Review*, January 30, 1955, p. 4, quoted in Baker, *Ernest Hemingway*, p. 647.

wise about people anyway, who said how, if you refused to accept something, it could not happen to you. And I was comforted.[16]

Hemingway, of course, never saw this screenplay.

By the time Hawks sold the rights on *To Have and Have Not* to Warner Brothers in October 1943, the project was well underway. Its first stage had been the working-out of that basic story line in 1939, and it is worth remembering that Hemingway and Hawks had agreed to throw out most of the novel and instead to tell the story of how Marie and Morgan might have met, with Hawks creating the character of Marie. Warners had assigned Humphrey Bogart to the picture early in 1943, but Hawks had been unable to cast Marie, and said so to his wife, Nancy "Slim" Hawks, one morning at breakfast. Slim, a former model and a prominent socialite, pointed to the photo on the cover of the current issue of *Harper's Bazaar* and suggested Hawks try out that model, one Betty Bacal. (Slim also discovered Joanne Dru and Ella Raines— each of whom, like Bacal, bore some physical resemblance to herself.)[17]

Hawks sent for the eighteen-year-old Bacal in April 1943 and spent several months training her. He was especially struck by the deep voice he was encouraging her to develop, and felt she might become another Dietrich. With that in mind, he told Jules Furthman—who had already begun work on the screenplay and who had written for Dietrich herself—to change the character of Marie, whom they were already calling Slim, into a sultry, almost masculine Dietrich type. When Bogart heard about these plans, Hawks told him he was "going to try and make a girl as insolent as you are." "Fat chance of that," said Bogart, and Hawks replied, "I've got a better than fat chance. . . . In every scene you play with her, she's going to walk out and leave you with egg on your face."[18] Shortly after she turned nineteen, Hawks changed her name to Lauren Bacall and wrote a scene for her screen test, which

16. George Sidney, "Faulkner in Hollywood: A Study of His Career as a Scenarist" (Ph.D. dissertation, University of New Mexico, 1959), p. 189.

17. "'Slim' Hawks," *Life*, January 20, 1947.

18. Joe Hyams, *Bogart and Bacall: A Love Story* (New York: Warner Books, 1976), pp. 60–68.

he shot early in January 1944. She leans against a door and says, "You know how to whistle, don't you? You just put your lips together and blow."[19] The rest, as they say, is history. Bacall so successfully dealt with the major challenge the role presented her (which was, as she later wrote, that of "trying to figure out how the hell a girl who was totally without sexual experience could convey experience, worldliness, and knowledge of men")[20] that Hawks told Furthman he could stop writing the script in two versions—one of which had a lesser role for Marie, in case the actress should prove too weak—and start working on a Final Screenplay. As matters between Bacall and Bogart developed, not even the Final allowed sufficient room for the romantic interest between Morgan and Marie to be dealt with. It is almost possible to organize all the versions of the script in terms of the gradually larger and more daring roles they offer Marie. But before we get too far ahead of ourselves, we should examine the story as Furthman originally wrote it.

The initial or Temporary Screenplay was completed by October 14, 1943.[21] It is both long (208 pages) and entertaining, and might even be called an adaptation of Hemingway's novel. It indicates how Hawks first conceived the project (there is no record of the Hemingway-Hawks treatment) and what Furthman contributed to the final product. For these reasons the plot line will be given below in some detail. First, however, a story that shows how Hawks and Furthman worked together, as well as some of the process that led to the character of Marie. This is the way Hawks told it:

Furthman could only work with Joe Sternberg, Vic Fleming, and myself. Everybody hated him so, but we sort of liked him because everybody hated him. . . . He was just obnoxious, [and] he had a strange life. He was married to a beautiful girl. They had a baby—turned out to be a moron—great *big* moron, didn't recognize anybody . . . and it would yell

19. Hyams, *Bogart and Bacall*, p. 73, and Bacall, *Lauren Bacall by Myself*, p. 90.

20. Bacall, *Lauren Bacall by Myself*, p. 91.

21. This is the date on which the script department finished copying the screenplay. The screenplay completion dates in the Inventory and throughout this Introduction should be taken in the same sense.

and everything. They had to move from a beautiful home in Bel Air, and he went down and bought some property outside Culver City. It turned out to be the most valuable manufacturing property there was. So he had a couple of million dollars worth of property. And if he didn't think anybody had any talent, Christ Almighty, he was a bad person to work for! He and Faulkner got on OK, but the average writer . . .

In *To Have and To Have Not* he wrote a story where Lauren Bacall has her purse stolen. He wrote a good scene about it and brought it in—very pleased with himself. "What do you think?" I said, "Well, Jules, there's a thing I always get a hard-on about—I get a complete erection for a little girl who's had her purse stolen." "You big son of a *bitch*," he said, and he stalked out and he came back the next day and wrote a scene where she stole a wallet. It was eight times as good. And I used to treat him that way, you know, to get him to work, because he did such damned fine work.

For the record, that "damned fine work" includes the screenplays for *Treasure Island* (1918), *Underworld* (1927), *The Drag Net* (1928), *The Docks of New York* (1928), *Morocco* (1930), *Shanghai Express* (1932), *Blonde Venus* (1932), *China Seas* (1935), *Mutiny on the Bounty* (1935), *Only Angels Have Wings* (1939), *The Shanghai Gesture* (1941), *The Outlaw* (1943), *The Big Sleep* (1946), *Nightmare Alley* (1947), *Rio Bravo* (1959), and more than eighty other films, either solo or in collaboration. Richard Corliss has described Furthman's recurring preoccupation as "the story of a grizzled adventurer who, with great exertions of will and the love of an equally adventurous woman, finds salvation for himself and those around him."[22] That is as good a description as any of *To Have and Have Not*, even though the film bears only occasional resemblance to Furthman's scripts for it.

Furthman's First Version

The Temporary Screenplay opens with Johnson's fishing scene. Apart from their being just outside the *Havana* harbor, Johnson's losing the two marlins and Morgan's tackle is played in the film

---

22. Richard Corliss, *Talking Pictures: Screenwriters in the American Cinema* (Baltimore: Penguin Books, 1975), p. 268.

basically as written here. Morgan's only crew member is Rummy (later Eddy), already endowed with his enigmatic line, "Was you ever bit by a dead bee?"

Back on the dock, Johnson reluctantly agrees to having the question of how much money he owes Morgan decided by Decimo and Benicia, the proprietors of the Pearl of San Francisco Cafe (Decimo becomes Frenchy/Gerard in the film; his wife, Benicia, an old flame of Morgan's, is dropped). They side with Morgan, and Johnson says he'll go to the bank the next day. Corinne (later Marie), a young woman who has been playing the cafe's piano and ordering rum swizzles while waiting for a nonexistent gentleman, picks up Johnson when Benicia threatens her with kitchen duty.

Later, Johnson collapses from too much liquor, and Corinne steals his wallet. Morgan corners her; they sarcastically call each other Steve and Slim, names neither of them likes. He has to slap her before she'll produce the wallet. They are interrupted (in a private dining room) by three Cuban students—Coyo, Florencio, and Pancho—who offer Morgan five thousand dollars to take them to Cienfuegos in his boat, apparently to rob a bank. Rummy comes in to tell Morgan that the boat has been attached until Morgan pays his local debts; he and the students go through the "drinking don't bother my memory" exchange. After Rummy leaves, the students ask Morgan whether he supports Machado, and he says, "It's nothing to do with me one way or another," but rejects the offer in the interests of personal safety and fear of losing his boat.

Morgan takes Corinne back to Johnson, intending to watch her return the wallet, but finds she has planted it in his own coat. Angry at Morgan, Johnson splits the wallet's contents with Corinne, then goes off with her to call the police. Outside the cafe, Pancho guns them down, having mistaken Johnson for Morgan. Johnson is killed, and Corinne's head is grazed. The killing is investigated by Lieutenant Caesar of the Havana police (Captain Renard in the film, although here he is "very slick and natty, carrying a brief case under his arm," and a friend of Morgan's). Because Corinne has a criminal record, Morgan hides her from Caesar; he also doesn't implicate the students. After Caesar leaves there is some business about the students' wanting to silence Corinne and Benicia's hoping they kill her.

Instead it turns out that the students have kidnapped Rummy. Morgan offers to trade them Corinne for his friend.[23] They say they'll keep Rummy and Corinne until Morgan drops them in Key West after the robbery. Florencio pulls a gun, and Morgan shoots him through the drawer of the table (more or less as in the film). Although uncontrollably angry at being pushed around, Morgan is convinced by Corinne and Benicia to let the others go, rather than kill them, so they can return Rummy.[24] By now Corinne and Benicia are friends.

The next day Mr. Kato (Mr. Sing in the novel) hires Morgan to smuggle a load of liquor to Florida that night. Rummy shows up; to get rid of him Morgan hits him hard and says, "You're poison to me." Morgan shoves off with a Negro crewman. Near dawn they are fired on by a Coast Guard cutter; the Negro is hit in the leg and Morgan in the arm. They are spotted again and not pursued (as in the novel—the other boat is captained by Morgan's friend). They decide to have a drink from the cargo and discover that they are actually carrying bottles filled with dope. Saying "what do I care about money? I got principle—" Morgan dumps the load overboard.

That night, in Morgan's bedroom, Corinne bandages his not-too-serious wound. Decimo brings in Kato; Morgan gives Kato the last bottle of morphine and arranges for Caesar to capture him with the evidence. Morgan goes downstairs and meets an American with his own set of tackle, Sam Essex, who charters his boat.

The next day, Sylvia ("a sleek, beautiful New Yorker"—later

23. Florencio observes that Morgan's decision proves that "A man who forms a tie is lost. No matter how great his courage. For he is no stronger than the thing he ties himself to." Decimo counters that such a man is "not lost, but safe. For no man is strong enough to look at life alone." This is the nearest Hawks and Furthman come to the sense of Morgan's dying words in the novel, and a bridge to the film's theme of the importance of personal and political commitment. It shows up in the film as the "no strings" exchange.

24. This ends the first of seven days. The film has a three-day plot, the novel three seasons.

Helene de Bursac, more or less) enters the cafe and recognizes Morgan. She turns out to be the "dame" in Morgan's past who soured him on women, the first woman who ever walked out on him—and married his best friend, Turner (now dead). Corinne and Benicia walk in; Morgan tells Sylvia that Corinne reminds him of her. "Where?" asks Sylvia. "Through the knees," says Morgan. There is a great deal of sparring until it is revealed that Essex is Sylvia's husband.[25] Essex comes in and announces that he has to fly to Key West on business, which postpones the fishing and incidentally gives Morgan and Sylvia the chance to have dinner and talk about old times, while the jealous Corinne gets drunk.

In the morning Corinne tries to explain to Rummy what a hangover is, then goes downstairs and makes friends with Sylvia. Essex shows up and Morgan arranges to take him fishing the next day. The students again kidnap Rummy, and Caesar indirectly helps Morgan free him—but the point has been made. To insure the safety of Rummy and Corinne, Morgan agrees to take the five revolutionaries (Pancho, Coyo, Enrico, Juan, and Esteban) on his boat. They apologize for applying such pressure, but insist that "the end justifies the means." Morgan observes that Machado said the same thing just the other day; as far as he's concerned, they should be fighting against the principle that "might is right." Juan

25. Not realizing that Turner has died, Morgan downplays the fact that he had left New York and become a fisherman in order to forget Sylvia, and pretends to be married and the father of two daughters. When he finds out that Turner is dead (of bleeding ulcers: "He insisted on keeping them for pets," says Sylvia. "He loved them and they loved him, I guess. Because one day they bled until he died for them"), Morgan admits he's single, kisses her roughly, and tries to leave with her. However, it seems that Sylvia herself was only playing "rich widow," for she is forced by Essex's entrance at this point to reveal that he is her husband. When Essex goes off to buy an antique fishing reel (he collects them), Sylvia gives Morgan enough information for him to figure out that Essex was *Turner's* best friend and that she was, therefore, basically responsible for her husband's death. She says Essex was the only man who could help her forget Morgan. Morgan realizes in a fury that she had tried to make *him* feel responsible for what she had done (contributed to the death of Turner, Morgan's best friend). Sylvia calms him down by suggesting they get together sometime. Corinne, who is as jealous as Benicia by now, tells Morgan he won't get any more credit at the cafe; Sylvia pays Morgan's sixty-five-dollar bill, giving Corinne a five-dollar tip. Corinne throws the money in her face, fights with Morgan, and is led off by Benicia. Enter Essex.

is moved by this argument ("If that is true, what have we to offer the people? Nothing but a change of masters"), but they all decide they'll have time to talk on the boat. Morgan tells them to seize his boat the next morning so that Essex can testify to Morgan's innocence.

The Cubans hijack Essex along with the boat. Morgan is surprised and angry to find that Rummy has stowed aboard too. Around noon they dock at Cienfuegos; four of the Cubans rob the bank while Juan keeps the boat covered. Morgan reassures Essex, who has been belowdecks vomiting from fear, that his reaction is normal (source of Morgan's fear-dialogue with the de Bursacs). The robbery is a success, but as they shove off Morgan needles Juan for allowing so much killing in the process.[26] Despite a passing impulse to shoot Morgan at this point, Juan says, "I wish you were on our side. You could go far with us. You have the quality to lead." "No thanks," says Morgan, "I haven't got the stomach for it." This exchange is significant as the climax of the political-involvement theme; it is very different from the film, since Morgan is asserting his moral convictions and abandoning his neutrality, and thereby *not* joining the anti-Fascists.[27]

Pancho goes belowdecks and finds that Rummy has drunk his special bottle of Fundador, so he grabs a machine gun and kills him at point-blank range (as with Albert in the novel).

Morgan and Essex make a plan. When Morgan goes up on deck to talk with the Cubans, Essex chokes the motor. To get Morgan to fix it, the Cubans pretend they will let Morgan kill Pancho. Morgan gets Coyo to help him throw Rummy's body overboard;

26. Juan explains, laughing, "They always get a little drunk when they kill so much. You know how it is." "I know how sharks get," says Morgan. Juan says that the other four are "good revolutionaries but very bad men" and admits that "when we come into power we will liquidate" the bad men whom they now need. Morgan laughs, and Juan draws a gun on him, saying he doesn't care what happens, Morgan can't laugh at his sacred cause (they need Morgan to run the boat). "Well," says Morgan, "that's different. When a man doesn't care about anything he's pretty hard to handle. I get that way myself sometimes." Juan smiles in admiration at Morgan's skillful reply.

27. In fact, the politics of the whole screenplay project a right-wing integration of imperialism and individualism, even though Machado is condemned throughout.

at the same time, Morgan kicks the machine gun into the sea (just as in the novel). This is noticed, but they still need him to fix the motor. In the engine room he signals the hidden Essex to open a valve, then gets out the small machine gun he had hidden. He returns to the deck and, asked whether everything's all right, says, "Everything is perfect." There is a fade out as he starts to fire.

The next morning Caesar lectures Morgan about trying to do everything on his own, tells him that the entire revolutionary group has been arrested or killed, and forgives Morgan's having taken the $825 Johnson owed him out of the bankroll.

Morgan then goes to the cafe, where he had sent advance word that he especially wants to see Slim (at the news, Corinne had cried for joy). Corinne tells him it was her fault Rummy died: she hadn't stopped him from sneaking off to the boat, because she knew how it felt to want to be with Morgan. Morgan goes upstairs for some sleep, but finds Sylvia in his room.

She tells him Essex will give him a job in New York and that she'll leave Essex to be with Morgan there. Morgan refuses, saying he really likes Essex now, but Sylvia realizes "it's that blonde inebriate." After she says this, she hits him in the face, then explains, "I had a feeling you were going to do it to me" and kisses the place. Then she suggests Morgan marry Corinne and bring her along, but he won't do that either, so Sylvia has Morgan unfasten her pearl necklace and tells him to give it to Corinne. "What's the idea?" asks Morgan, and Sylvia closes the script with these splendid lines: "I don't know. (Kissing him, she looks into his eyes, gay and insolent as ever.) 'The robbed who smiles steals something from the thief.' (Then, turning and picking up her hat.) Shakespeare."[28]

The most important difference between the Temporary Screenplay and the novel is that here, whatever losses Morgan suffers are reversible, whereas what Hemingway showed was an inexorable process of one loss's leading to another until Morgan was destroyed. In the novel Morgan's being cheated by Johnson makes it impossible for him to earn his living as a fisherman; his

28. *Othello* act 1, sc. 3, l. 208.

smuggling run results in the loss of his arm and boat; reduced at last to dealing with revolutionaries, he gets killed. Of course Hawks wanted to tell a story of how Morgan and Marie might have met, and would hardly have felt it appropriate to kill off the hero—but even beyond that, Hawks had a temperamental objection to stories about, as he put it, losers. So in the first screenplay Morgan goes through the same basic sequence of situations (Johnson, smuggling, revolutionaries) and ends up with a wife, a healed arm, and the money Johnson owed him—his only loss being Rummy. (Hawks followed this same principle of adaptation on *The Big Sleep*.) By the same token, the theme of the isolated hero is redeemed by reversal: Hawks and Furthman show how Morgan discovers that men must fight together in order to win (i.e., he needs Essex and Caesar to beat the revolutionaries, and the revolutionaries falter because they distrust each other), but on the other hand they present Morgan as doing a pretty good job on his own anyway.

A number of other basic transitions from the novel to the film are begun or established here. The character of Eddy/Rummy is hardly changed from here on, though he is of course not killed in the film. Marie/Corinne is an odd mix of drunk, tramp, and insolent princess. Morgan has been recast for Bogart. Decimo and Juan are ready to be melded into Frenchy/Gerard. A cafe/hotel/bar has been made the major location of off-seas action. And there is an attempt at retaining the novel's double focus (Cuba and the eastern U.S. establishment) via Essex and Sylvia; this doubleness, however, is well on the way to being the simple love triangle (Morgan, Marie, and Helene) that dominates Furthman's later scripts as well as the press releases for the film (which made much of Bogart's being chased by two blondes—Bacall and Dolores Moran). In the film, Sylvia survives only in Marie's lines, "Who was the girl, Steve . . . ? The one who left you with such a high opinion of women." Sylvia's sexy wit is transferred to Marie (or dropped), and Helene gets the pearl necklace.

The good cop becomes a bad cop when the film takes on a different set of Fascists. There is little focus to the Temporary Screenplay's politics beyond a distrust of terrorist priorities. Morgan doesn't care one way or the other about Machado, but he has sufficient "principle" to dump the load of morphine and turn Kato over to the police. Despite Caesar's lectures on political change and solidarity, the important ties Morgan discovers are those of love (Corinne) and friendship (Rummy). This most problematic area of the adaptation is resolved by the later decision to model much of *To Have and Have Not* on *Casablanca* (1942)—not just because it raised no political ambivalence to oppose the Vichy during wartime, but also because *Casablanca* had shown how the Bogart persona could be led into a clear political stance by considerations of love and friendship. All this is a further side effect of the change of story locale from Cuba to Martinique, from Machado to Vichy.

Furthman's Revisions

Furthman's Revised Temporary Screenplay, which was generated in case Bacall should turn out to be unable to handle a starring role,[29] was left unfinished (at 111 pages) before January 5, 1944. In this version the character and functions of Corinne are split between Marie and Amelia, who is Morgan's American girlfriend. Sylvia is renamed Helen Gordon and has no husband. Rummy is Eddy, and the Negro bait cutter, Wesley (later Horatio), is introduced. There is a piano player, Chuck (later Cricket), working for Decimo and Benicia. Johnson is killed accidentally during a street battle between two revolutionary factions. Lieutenant Caesar, who is now a chubby fellow in charge of the secret police, and not Morgan's friend, is still full of theories about what it takes to make "an honest revolution." Morgan has two smuggling scenes (basically as in the novel): in the first he kills Kato and sets the Japanese—not Chinese—ashore; in the second he receives a serious arm wound and dumps the load of liquor overboard.

Furthman wrote the Final Screenplay in January and early February, and completed it before February 14, 1944. It is 151 pages long, and may have been the direct source for Faulkner's shooting script (the Second Revised Final, printed in this volume). There was a Revised Final, signed by Furthman and dated February 18, 1944 (discovered in the University of Southern California Library

29. Hyams, *Bogart and Bacall*, p. 70.

by Holly Yasui), but for reasons explained in the Foreword, page 8, I haven't been allowed to examine it. Other materials that are undoubtedly relevant but unavailable at this time include extensive notes and drafts of scenes written for Hawks during January and February of 1944 by the mystery writer Cleve F. Adams. In one letter I did see, Adams asks Hawks whether he ought to keep writing independently of someone named Chambers, or begin to collaborate with him. These materials are on deposit at the USC Library.

The account of the Cuba-to-Martinique change that is presented in this introduction is a reconstruction based on more than a year of research. My basic conclusion is that Faulkner was responsible for many of these changes and is the sole author of the Second Revised Final. I am especially indebted to Meta Carpenter Wilde, who was script girl on the picture, for her clear memory of Faulkner's contribution to the project. Hawks took credit for the change to an anti-Vichy story, though he says the censors suggested the Martinique location. The Second Revised Final bears the names of Furthman (typed) and Faulkner (in a bold handwriting that is not Faulkner's). The Adams scenes were apparently generated as alternatives to some of Furthman's before the locale was changed; no one seems to know anything about Chambers. It seems likely that Furthman's Revised Final was the actual script from which Faulkner worked, and that since Furthman worked on that Revised Final for only four days, it did not differ considerably from the Final discussed here. So it is proper to say that Furthman and Faulkner wrote the screenplay of *To Have and Have Not*, so long as one remembers that they did not work together. Furthman remained on the payroll but did no writing after Faulkner was brought on the job.

The Final is full of interesting and significant changes; it is still a complex and somewhat redundant story, however, and I offer some of it in detail as a way of showing both what Faulkner had to work with and how economically he restructured and clarified that material. (It is of course no secret that Faulkner was a great writer and a master of construction, but it is good to have evidence of his having applied those skills in Hollywood.)

Although Amelia and Benicia are still present in the Final, they play relatively minor roles, and it is clear that by this time "that kid from New York" had the role of Marie and that Furthman and Hawks were writing whole scenes for her. Helen Gordon is an important figure, but the Dietrich-like Marie is for the first time her match. The screen test Hawks had written for Bacall ("You know how to whistle") here appears for the first time, and Marie is even given a line lifted directly from *Shanghai Express* (1932; directed by Von Sternberg, written by Furthman, and starring Dietrich). In that film, when Shanghai Lily is interrogated as to her reasons for going to Shanghai, she answers, "To buy a new hat"; Marie here says this to Captain Renardo, Lieutenant Caesar's nasty assistant, during the investigation of Johnson's death (much as in the film). Other changes:

The Final begins with a dock scene rather than with the catching of the first marlin. When Morgan and Johnson go to the cafe, they find Cricket at the piano and Marie humming along. Morgan is established as a man who refuses to borrow money and will not even accept a free meal. Later that night, when Morgan examines the wallet Marie has stolen from Johnson, he finds a plane ticket and nine hundred dollars in traveler's checks. The student revolutionaries are friends of Decimo's, and when Morgan refuses to take them to Cienfuegos he does wish them luck. Marie does not frame Morgan when he makes her return the wallet. Johnson is killed during a battle between the students who have just left Morgan and the police (Renardo and Coyo); the only student to escape is Pancho. Renardo interrogates Morgan and Marie and slaps them both; Caesar (Morgan's friend again) intervenes and insults Renardo for killing a tourist during racing season; for the first time, Caesar keeps the contents of Johnson's wallet for evidence. Leaving Eddy with Amelia, Morgan escorts Marie to her hotel (only in Faulkner's version do they stay in the same hotel), where they decide to have a drink in the basement cafe and Marie has to hustle a bottle. In her room they go through what will become the most famous scene in the film, from "You're sore, aren't you?" to the whistle line, with the difference that Morgan does accept her cash reserve (which he uses the next day to buy her a ticket home); also, the whistle line is intended to be bitter, as the climax to Marie's developing feeling of cheapness.

Introduction

Morgan agrees to take Kato's Japanese cargo. He gives Marie her ticket and goes to his room, where he finds Eddy asleep and Helen Gordon taking a shower. Helen's current husband is divorcing her in Reno; it is established that Helen married two fishermen on Morgan's account and that Morgan was with Benicia before he was with Helen. Marie gets a job singing in the cafe. That night Morgan kills Kato and gets the Japanese ashore; Eddy has stowed aboard despite Morgan's hitting and insulting him. Morgan uses Kato's money to buy a load of liquor, which he dumps after he and Wesley are shot.

Recuperating in Marie's room, Morgan calls her his "Jonah"; in his delirium he speaks his dying lines from the novel (slightly censored). Pancho brings a leftist physician, and in a few days Morgan recovers; by that time Helen and Marie are friends. Marie urges Morgan to help Pancho rather than fly off to New York with Helen like a quitter. What convinces him is her saying *she's* not leaving Havana until she's licked, and that it was Pancho and not Decimo (as Morgan had assumed) who brought the doctor.

Pancho insists that he and Morgan carry Eddy along with them to Cienfuegos (where they will pick up the four bank robbers), since he knows so much about their plans. One of the robbers kills Eddy when he makes a fuss about picking them up. Pancho realizes that now they will have to kill Morgan too, but Morgan stalls and that night kills all of them with his hidden gun. The next day Morgan turns the money (from "Machado's private bank") over to Caesar and says the revolution needs not "crooks or fanatics" but men like Caesar who have cool heads and love Cuba; otherwise "they're going to end up with something just as bad as the thing they're trying to bust."

Morgan returns to the cafe, where Helen is packing his things; they are going to fly to New York, where Helen intends to sell her property so that she and Morgan can marry and live in Havana. Just before they get on the seaplane Morgan changes his mind, and Helen gives him the pearl necklace to give to Marie.

So by the middle of February 1944, Hawks and Furthman had put together a witty and elaborate script, telling the story of how Morgan and Marie might have met, and retaining from the novel

30

Johnson's fishing trip, Mr. Sing/Kato's alien-smuggling operation, Morgan's arm wound, and the bank robbery, together with some commentary on Machado and the coming revolution. Then came what Hawks described to the *New York Times* as "a modern Hollywood version of a Tinker-to-Evers-to-Chance triple play."[30]

Enter Faulkner

The Office of the Coordinator of Inter-American Affairs suddenly objected to Warner Brothers' plans to film a novel that might embarrass the Batista regime in Cuba. Although *To Have and Have Not* concerns the Machado regime, it was felt that the project featured smuggling and insurrection in a way that would reflect badly on Cuba no matter when the story was set. It seems clear from this distance that what really motivated that cleverly reasoned objection was the Batista regime's recognizing its kinship with the Machado regime (not its fear that it would be mistaken for Machado's kin, in other words, but the true and undiscussable contemporaneity of the story).

The specific way that Office applied pressure was to predict that the picture would not receive an export license from the Office of Censorship. Without such a license, it would be almost impossible for the picture to earn much money, since it could not be shown overseas. The United States and Cuba were allies in the current war effort, and the United States was at this point interested more in supporting and receiving the sugar crop than in implying that Cuba could stand another revolution.

Since the Cuban setting was ruled out, Jack Warner told Hawks they could not do the picture, even though some of the sets had been built, second-unit photography had already started, and close to a million dollars had been invested. Hawks asked the Inter-American Affairs Office whether it could suggest another location (much as he later asked the censors to come up with an acceptable ending for *The Big Sleep*), and it told him that the French territory of Martinique was outside its sphere of concern.

30. Fred Stanley, "Hollywood Report," *New York Times*, April 2, 1944.

At that point Hawks asked his friend Faulkner for advice, as he often did when he was having trouble with a scene or story.[31] Faulkner had been on the payroll at Warner Brothers since 1942 (when he helped Hawks with two scenes for *Air Force*) and in 1942–43 had written an anti-Vichy screenplay—"The De Gaulle Story," excerpted above—which Warners had decided not to produce. Faulkner suggested that *To Have and Have Not* be rewritten so that the political interest would be the conflict between the Free French and the Vichy government, and Hawks hired him to do the job on February 22, 1944. Although Hawks himself took credit for thinking of this change, Meta Carpenter Wilde (Hawks's script girl and, intermittently, Faulkner's lover) has emphatically vouched that the idea was Faulkner's.[32] By saving this picture, Faulkner markedly advanced his reputation as a professional screenwriter.

The government, however, was not through yet. As the *New York Times* put it, "Since the new treatment involved Europe and the present war, the picture immediately became the concern of the Overseas Branch of the Office of War Information. Furthermore, because of the over-all character of the subject and the possibility of Production Code infraction in regard to the treatment of foreigners, the Hays office was brought into the picture. Now, as the script is being written, just ahead of production, individual scenes are sent to all three offices for review and suggestions."[33] Faulkner's scenes were written, on an average, three days before being shot. For such a shy and autonomous artist, this ought to have been an impossible working situation, but Faulkner managed to please everyone concerned and still write a good script, one that does, thirty-six years later, merit publication on its own.

The first cast reading took place on March 6, 1944, and the last script changes are dated April 22; shooting was completed on May 10. Although this last-minute writing gave Faulkner an unusual

31. See Bruce Kawin, "Faulkner's Film Career: The Years with Hawks," in Evans Harrington and Ann J. Abadie, eds., *Faulkner, Modernism, and Film* (Jackson: University Press of Mississippi, 1979), for details of their relationship, most of it from Hawks's point of view. For a list of Faulkner's screenplays, see Bruce Kawin, "A Faulkner Filmography," *Film Quarterly* 30 (Summer 1977): 12–21.

32. Unpublished interview between Mrs. Wilde and myself on June 20, 1978.

33. *New York Times*, April 2, 1944.

amount of control over the final product—it would have been virtually impossible for Hawks to *restructure* his script under these conditions—there were a great many changes *within* the scenes, as the Notes section of this volume demonstrates. In an interview Bogart gave late that April, he said that Faulkner, Hawks, and himself were devising new scenes, dialogue, and gags as they went along, on the set; he made no mention of Furthman, who was still on the payroll but—according to Mrs. Wilde and others— not doing any writing.[34] In her autobiography Bacall says that Bogart and Hawks revised much of the dialogue and that Faulkner preferred to remain in Hawks's office.[35] Most of these on-the-set changes had the effect of making the characters less "literary" in feel, more in harmony with their established screen personalities— but there were substantial changes too, particularly in the treatment of women. These will be discussed shortly.

Hawks said that Faulkner enjoyed changing Hemingway's material just because it was Hemingway's. In fact, Faulkner seems to have had little interest in that aspect of the project, and was more interested in the political aspects of the script; his personal interest was in helping his friend Hawks out of a jam. His anti-Vichy sentiments are evident in the comic tone of the opening scene and the serious tone of the closing, as well as in his treatment of the de Bursacs and Captain Renard (who are not simply lifted from *Casablanca*, although it might seem that way at first). In a letter written to his agent, Faulkner revealed no enthusiasm for the script he was writing, did not even mention Hemingway, and concentrated on the difficulty of doing good work while there was anything as serious as a war going on:

As soon as I got here, Howard Hawks asked for me. He is making a picture at our shop. As usual, he had a script, threw it away and asked for me. I went to work helping to rewrite it about Feb. 22. He started shooting about Mar. 1. Since then I have been trying to keep ahead of him with a day's script. I should be through about May 10–15.

I dont know when I shall get back at it [i.e., his novel, *A Fable*]. . . . War is bad for writing, though why I should tell you. This sublimation

34. *New York Herald Tribune*, April 30, 1944.
35. Bacall, *Lauren Bacall by Myself*, pp. 95–96.

and glorification of all the cave instincts which man had hopes that he had lived down, dragged back into daylight, usurping pre-empting a place, all the room in fact, in the reality and constancy and solidity of art, writing. Something must give way; let it be the writing, art, it has happened before, will happen again. . . .

When and if I get at it again, I will write you. After being present for a while at the frantic striving of motion pictures to justify their existence in a time of strife and terror, I have about come to the conclusion which they dare not admit: that the printed word and all its ramifications and photographications is nihil nisi fui; in a word, a dollar mark striving frantically not to DISSOLVE into the symbol 1A.[36]

This is hardly an inspiring mood, and the closing joke reflects badly on the studio's pious propaganda efforts. It seems that Faulkner put his anti-Vichy sentiments into the script and saved his antiwar sentiments for *A Fable*; he was also evidently still upset about never having been in combat himself.

Despite all this ambivalence, Faulkner did a solid and professional job on the Second Revised Final. Most of his changes will be evident to the reader, but a few of them merit mention here. He developed Helen Gordon into Helene de Bursac, Caesar and Renardo into Captain Renard, Decimo into Gerard, Pancho into Beauclerc, and the Cuban revolutionaries into the supporters of de Gaulle. He turned Morgan from patient to physician. He let Eddy survive. He dropped Benicia and Amelia, Frankie (a go-between) and Mr. Kato, the bank robbery, both smuggling scenes, all of Morgan's immoral actions, and the whole question of the legitimacy of the anti-Fascist cause. He made the relationship between Morgan and Eddy more tender. He took aspects of the de Bursacs (agitators in hiding, male-oriented wife) from *Casablanca*. He left Marie as Morgan's only love-interest—although he apparently could not resist turning Morgan into something of a misogynist; Morgan's washing off Helene's perfume in scene 45, for ex-

---

36. Joseph Blotner, ed., *Selected Letters of William Faulkner* (New York: Random House, 1977), pp. 180–81. The letter is dated April 22, so my guess is that between then and May 10 he expected to work mostly on last-minute, on-the-set changes. © 1977 by Jill Faulkner Summers. Reprinted by permission of Random House, Inc.

ample, is similar to Marlowe's reaction to Carmen Sternwood in a scene Faulkner wrote for *The Big Sleep*,[37] and Morgan is given numerous lines hostile to women. (He behaves this way neither in Furthman's scripts nor in the film.) Faulkner also played down the theme of Morgan's compulsive independence (whose only vestige in the film is Morgan's refusing Marie's offer of her safety money), made Marie less of a drinker, shortened the story to three days (a major improvement), and firmed up both the plot and its logistics by having Morgan and Marie take rooms in the same hotel. This is, on the whole, the most serious in tone and purpose of all the scripts, as well as the most economically constructed.

Faulkner was apparently not upset at Hawks's changing it, line by line, into a more sexually affirmative, upbeat comedy. Since both the shooting script and a list of significant alterations in the dialogue are available in this volume, I will cite here only a few examples of Hawks's revisions, which may clarify the logic of the others.

The most general rule Hawks followed, besides that of springing a new scene on his actors for the fun of it, was to let a line-change stand if the new version sounded more natural for that actor. In scene 12, for instance, Morgan's "Don't make me feel bad" becomes "Well, boys, don't make me feel bad." If he felt the rhythm of a scene falling, Hawks would rearrange the dialogue into his own "three-cushion" style, full of interruptions and overlapping lines. Here is part of Faulkner's scene 46:

EDDY: Listen, Harry. Could I—?
MORGAN: You've had enough to last you a week. (To Marie.) Don't buy him nothing but beer.
(As he turns to go Frenchy enters.)
MORGAN: Have any trouble getting them ashore?
FRENCHY: No. But Madame refused to let us take them to that place in the country. She said it was too far. He would die before he got there.
MORGAN: What does she know?
FRENCHY: He is very badly wounded, Harry. Anybody can see that.

37. Kawin, *Faulkner and Film*, p. 118.

Here is the Hawks version:

EDDY: Harry, we can use—
MORGAN: She'll buy it for you. Nothin' but beer for him, Slim.
MARIE: I'll remember. We'll be all right, Steve. I've got a job.
MORGAN: Doin' what?
MARIE: Frenchy seems to think I can sing.
MORGAN: Well, it's his place.
MARIE: Sometimes you make me so mad I could—
GERARD: Harry!
MORGAN: You could do what?
MARIE: I could—
GERARD: Harry, I need your help.
MORGAN: Well, what is it now?
GERARD: That— (indicating Marie—an "is she one of us?" look.)
MORGAN: That's all right. Go ahead.
GERARD: That man is very badly wounded, Harry.

The reader will note also the deletion of Morgan's "What does she know?"

There are changes in tone throughout. When Marie exits on her whistle line (after Hawks has rearranged the elements of the scene so that it is less moody and more tongue-in-cheek), Morgan whistles. Or in scene 53, when Marie says, "Give her my love" (meaning Helene), Morgan answers, "I'd give her my own if she had that on" (meaning Marie and her dress), rather than simply looking at her over his shoulder. There is considerable toning-down of Faulkner's longer passages on patriotism and fear (especially in scene 54), and nearly all of Helene's serious lines and erratic behavior are cut out—in favor of a new scene where she offers Morgan her jewels (a holdover from Sylvia/Helen Gordon and her pearl necklace). There is a great deal of downright good-naturedness written in, too, as when Morgan tells Frenchy's cashier that he'll still owe her the hotel bill even after he's fixed Paul's wound (this might have been played as an indication of Morgan's refusal to accept help, but that was clearly neither its intention nor its effect). But the simplest way to conceptualize these changes is to compare Faulkner's and Hawks's closing scenes. Faulkner makes it clear that the theme he announced in his opening—resistance to Vichy—is the major one in the picture, and closes with Frenchy's going upstairs to kill the policemen while Cricket makes enough racket to cover the shooting. (It is common for Faulkner's scripts to end at some tense moment that precedes a resolution.) Hawks, on the other hand, ends with Marie and Eddy's bebopping out of the cafe with Morgan while Cricket strikes up a jazzy exit (that seques into "How Little We Know," the main romantic theme, played by a studio orchestra under the final title card).[38]

Fun on the Set

During the fairly leisurely nine weeks of shooting (March 6 to May 10) the mood on the set ranged from the congenial to the electric, with most of the electricity being generated by and around Bogart and Bacall. Both of them were under stress much of the time. In addition to the predictable anxieties associated with playing a major role in her first film, Bacall felt it necessary to conceal from both Hawks and Bogart, until well after the picture was completed, the fact that she was a Jew (both men made casual anti-Semitic remarks);[39] it seems, in fact, that she kept this secret long after it was not a secret. Bogart had more serious problems: he was married to a wildly violent alcoholic, and his own drinking was entirely out of control. His home life consisted mainly of intense arguments; his wife, Mayo, often threw lamps, etc., once even knifed him in the back, and resented his professional success whenever her own acting career was doing poorly.[40] They were known as the Battling Bogarts, and it was Hawks's opinion as well as that of some of their friends that they were well matched.

The working day was usually divided in three: first, rewriting and blocking the scene; second, lunch—usually a chance for Hawks and Furthman to confer on horses and place their bets; third, shooting. This is Bacall's account of the process:

Howard had a brilliantly creative work method. Each morning when we got to the set, he, Bogie, and I and whoever else might be in the scene,

---

38. In addition, Hawks has Frenchy decide not to kill the policemen; see note 120.

39. Hyams, *Bogart and Bacall*, p. 95; Bacall, *Lauren Bacall by Myself*, p. 95.

40. Hyams, *Bogart and Bacall*, pp. 75–82; Bacall, *Lauren Bacall by Myself*, p. 98.

and the script girl would sit in a circle in canvas chairs with our names on them and read the scene. Almost unfailingly Howard would bring in additional dialogue for the scenes of sex and innuendo between Bogie and me. After we'd gone over the words several times and changed whatever Bogie or Howard thought should be changed, Howard would ask an electrician for a work light—one light on the set—and we'd go through the scene on the set to see how it felt. Howard said, "Move around—see where it feels most comfortable." Only after all that had been worked out did he call Sid Hickox and talk about camera set-ups. It is the perfect way for movie actors to work, but of course it takes time.[41]

There were exceptions to this process, and not all shooting was done after lunch, but the general rule was that Hawks shot his films at a leisurely (and therefore expensive) pace. He kept a yellow pad on his lap throughout the working day so that he could write new scenes—"to upset the actors," as he put it. This both amused him and increased his control over the actors. But the developing romance between his stars proved a serious challenge to that control.

He was later to claim that he exploited the attraction between Bogart and Bacall, using it to improve the scenes rather than fighting it. He said that his problem was that he couldn't "get them to pay attention." It is certainly true that he decided in midstream to reduce the script's emphasis on Dolores Moran (Helene), realizing that there was no point in trying to work a love triangle into the story since the audience would never take it seriously.[42] In her autobiography, however, Bacall reveals another side to this story.[43] Apparently Hawks had always wanted to play Svengali to some ingenue actress, and he became furious—perhaps even jealous—at Bacall's refusal to make work the focus of her life. He told her Bogart was simply toying with her and that her concentration was suffering. "I'm not going to put up with it," he told her one night at his house. "I tell you I'll just send you to Monogram. I'll wash my hands of you." (Monogram was Hawks's idea of a bottom-of-the-barrel studio; although it is dear to the hearts of many

41. Bacall, *Lauren Bacall by Myself*, p. 96.
42. Bacall, *Lauren Bacall by Myself*, p. 104.
43. Bacall, *Lauren Bacall by Myself*, pp. 77–129, esp. pp. 99 and 123.

B-movie fans, Bacall seems to have regarded it as an outer chamber of Hell.) This threat so upset her that she and Bogart hid the relationship from Hawks until they were well into *The Big Sleep*; once the story did come out, Hawks never again worked with either of them.

Another aspect of Hawks's controlling behavior is that he refused to work while Jack Warner was on the set; this practice was all to the good, since Warner was by all accounts a hostile, meddling, and at times downright stupid person. There's a wonderful story about Warner's sending Hawks a telegram during the shooting of *The Big Sleep*: "Word has reached me that you are having fun on the set. This must stop."[44] They apparently had fun on the set of *To Have and Have Not* as well. On the slapstick side, Dolores Moran got lost in the fog during the shooting of the scene where Morgan first picks up the de Bursacs; she walked off a jetty into the waist-deep studio lake. Hoagy Carmichael, the composer of "Stardust," kept a match in his mouth during most of his scenes; he had never acted before, and this prop, everyone assured him, helped make his characterization "distinctive." The way a press release told the story, Carmichael "came on the set one day to see Humphrey Bogart rehearsing a scene—and nonchalantly chewing on a match. Bogart is the star of the film, so Carmichael suffered in silence and finally left before the scene was shot. He returned an hour later. Walter Brennan was rehearsing a scene. At its most dramatic moment, he took a large kitchen match from his pocket, and casually put it between his lips." Later Bogart explained it was all a hoax.

Hawks and Bogart served as their own technical advisers for much of the picture. Hawks was a champion game-fisherman, and Bogart, who loved the sea, was devoted to sailing, so the scenes on Morgan's boat were carefully and naturally played (despite some obvious rear-projection work in Johnson's fishing scene). One press release describes Hawks and Bogart's examining a shotgun to be used in one of the scenes: "'It's a beauty,' commented Hawks, who rates as one of Hollywood's top shotgun and rifle marksmen. 'Yeah,' agreed Bogart, 'it looks all right, but I

44. Bacall, *Lauren Bacall by Myself*, p. 121.

really wouldn't know about it. I'm a machine-gun man, myself.'" To establish the proper angle of the bullet-effect during the scene where Morgan shoots one of Renard's men through the drawer of a table, Bogart insisted on going outside and shooting "a real slug through the thing."[45] (The publicity for the picture emphasized this sort of "man's man" aspect of Hawks and especially Bogart. Not only was Bacall touted—in advance—as a major discovery, but her and Moran's screen interest in Bogart/Morgan was described as the "Battle of the Blondes.")

Bogart and Hawks worked closely on dialogue changes, as has been said before, and it is worth calling attention to two further aspects of their working relationship: they agreed on matters of "good taste," and trusted each other's judgment. One Warner Brothers press release quotes Bogart to the effect that he felt comfortable in making suggestions to Hawks about how to play a certain scene, that "a good director is like a good psychiatrist; he builds up the confidence of his players until they forget their fears and inhibitions," and that he trusted Hawks to "correct" him if he was "off the beam." He went on to say that "whether a scene calls for you to kiss a girl or kill a man, the element of good taste is vital. The killing scene may be shocking to sensibilities without being offensive to good taste. That goes double for kiss scenes."

This issue of tastefulness has a great deal to do with the excellence of Hawks's style as both producer and director, from his choice of camera angles and wardrobes to his guiding concepts of professionalism and love. He had clear ideas of how things ought to be done, and the people he worked with trusted him.

Hawks described a good director as "somebody who doesn't annoy you."[46] He felt he put the camera in the obvious place it should be. He lit to clarify rather than overstate mood. All this makes his pictures so classical that they are nearly impossible to analyze—they are simply done "correctly." Bogart's comment re-

45. This and other press releases referred to in this section are undated and come from the press book file on the picture.
46. Robin Wood, *Howard Hawks* (Garden City, N.Y.: Doubleday, 1968), p. 11. When I asked Hawks what he considered the best book written about him, he singled out Robin Wood's; it is, unfortunately, out of print. (It is vol. 7 in the *Cinema World* series.) On the unanalyzability of Hawks's work, see pp. 10–11.

veals that actors relied on Hawks to "correct" them—in other words, to bring out the *right* performance; this is a very different matter from that of making sure one is doing whatever the director, who may be capricious or on a very private track, happens to have in mind. And this is an important aspect of what Hawks meant by "professional": not just a skillful or efficient manner of proceeding, but the obviously proper way to get the job done (an attitude that usually carries with it a set of ethics).

Hawks did not intellectualize his approach to cinema. His way of explaining what he did was that he and his actors and writers simply "had fun," tried things out to see what was "comfortable," behaved "professionally," didn't "annoy" the audience. His ethics were similarly unexamined: pride led to a fall, love healed, good work prospered—in *Red River*, for instance—not because Hawks got these concepts out of a manual on Greek and Latin literature but because he was himself a classical artist and a man with a secure world view.

He never did understand what the French critics saw in his work; he was convinced they were reading in meanings he never intended, and so on. (Not that he was modest—he was more than willing to take credit for the things he had done. He recognized, for instance, that no matter how often Orson Welles said he learned directing from screening *Stagecoach*, *Citizen Kane* was much more closely modeled on *His Girl Friday*—and furthermore, said Welles had told him so in 1941.)[47] But one can be a master without being self-conscious about it; one can achieve brilliant results while setting out simply to have fun and do a good job, without being dismissed as a lucky innocent. Perhaps the preceding discussion of his working methods on *To Have and Have Not* may help to clarify the personal and professional sources of Hawks's uniquely clean, efficient, entertaining, and classical style. His assured sense of control, his relative independence from Jack Warner (at least in matters not involving the government), his ability to work with the censors, his manner of dealing with writers (goading Hemingway, teasing Furthman, respecting Faulk-

47. This was the story with which Hawks ended our 1976 interview.

ner), his encouraging his actors to trust him and to feel comfortable coupled with his insistence that they pay careful attention to his demands, his taking a firm hand in everything from setting the camera angles and approving all production details to designing the plot and revising the script day by day—certainly all this contributed to the excellence of the final product as well as to its coherence. In the case of a work as capriciously conceived and continually interfered with as *To Have and Have Not*, that coherence may be its most remarkable feature. Such apparent seamlessness as the final work manifests is one of the marks of great art, and it seems proper at this point to introduce a judgment by one of the cinema's most literate and intense observers.

When he was just starting out as a critic for *Cahiers* (in 1952), Jean-Luc Godard pronounced Hawks the greatest American artist, and although that has to be considered an overstatement, Godard does make a good case:

There is a famous legend which has it that Griffith, moved by the beauty of his leading lady, invented the close-up in order to capture it in greater detail. Paradoxically, therefore, the simplest close-up is also the most moving. Here our art reveals its transcendence most strongly, making the beauty of the object signified burst forth in the sign. . . . Where Preminger uses a crane, Hawks is apt to use an axial cut: the means of expression change only because the subjects change, and the sign draws its signification not from itself but from what it represents, from the scene enacted. . . . All I mean to claim is that the *mise en scène* of *To Have and Have Not* is better suited than that of *The Best Years of Our Lives* to convey aberrations of heart and mind, that this is its purpose, whereas the object of the latter is rather the external relationships between people. . . . Certainly one has only to consider the development of the greatest American artist—I mean Howard Hawks—to see how relative this idea of classicism is. From the art of *Only Angels Have Wings* to that of *His Girl Friday*, *The Big Sleep* and indeed, of *To Have and Have Not*, what does one see? An increasingly precise taste for analysis, a love for this artificial grandeur connected to movements of the eyes, to a way of walking, in short, a greater awareness than anyone else of what the cinema can glory in, and a refusal to profit from this (as I would accuse Orson Welles of doing in *Macbeth*, and Robert Bresson in *Journal d'un curé de campagne*) to create anti-

Introduction

cinema, but instead, through a more rigorous knowledge of its limits, fixing its basic laws.[48]

The only sense in which Godard and I differ here is in our uses of the term "classical": he is referring to a set of conventions within the history of narrative film, and I am referring to a set of structural and ethical assumptions that date back to ancient times. I consider it no accident that Hawks was able to work well with authors of Faulkner's stature, nor that he was the first producer to select a Conrad work for adaptation;[49] his work does demand to be set in the largest possible artistic context. So although I consider Faulkner, Melville, Whitman, Keaton, Gertrude Stein, and a few others to be more likely candidates for the no doubt pointless distinction "greatest American artist," I believe Godard is right to put Hawks in the company of our major creative figures.

The Film and Its Reception

The most accomplished characteristic of Hawks's films is their rhythm, and *To Have and Have Not* shows this aspect of his work at its best. It marks the balance point of his range, which extends from the rapid-fire overlapping dialogue of *His Girl Friday* to the more slow and elegant structural repetitions of *Hatari!* It is not just a matter of the meter and pace of dialogue, but of the way dialogue, music, camera position, and actor movement are gracefully coordinated. There are times when it seems as if Hawks invented the sound film, or at least brought it to perfection—particularly in his first two pictures with Faulkner, *Today We Live* (1933) and *The Road to Glory* (1936). One elegant, easy-to-take example of Hawks's mastery is the script's scene 10 (notes 25 and 26). In its two and a half minutes of screen time, Hawks establishes the attraction be-

48. Jean-Luc Godard, "Defence and Illustration of Classical Construction," in *Godard on Godard*, ed. Jean Narboni and Tom Milne (New York: Viking, 1972), pp. 28–30.

49. When he was a fledgling producer at Famous Players–Lasky, around 1924, Hawks prepared approximately forty pictures a year. During one of those years he produced two Zane Greys and two Joseph Conrads. He didn't tell me the titles, but he did say he was the first person in pictures to have read so widely. One of those Conrads has to have been *Lord Jim* (1925), directed by Victor Fleming.

tween Morgan and Marie, shows Johnson's pawing Marie and her stealing his wallet, takes care of the script's basic business between Morgan and Frenchy, and has Cricket sing an entire song—all of this done so fluidly, so assuredly, with each event swinging its partner as if in a Virginia reel, that the sequence does not even feel fast. What goes before is that Morgan, in his room, tells Frenchy he will not help the radicals (a few seconds after Marie has exited with her lit cigarette). As Morgan closes the door, there is a dissolve to:

[Shot 1] Mid-shot of the bar; two men talking; a waitress walks between the men, holding her tray; the camera follows her to one of the tables and stops panning as we see Morgan sitting alone at a table in the background. The camera tracks forward until Morgan is in close-up in the center of the screen. He strikes a match to light his cigarette, and the music starts.

[Shot 2] Long shot, Morgan's point-of-view; Cricket and his piano are in the center of the screen; Johnson and Marie are at a table, screen left, drinking. (In context this is almost an extreme long shot.)

[Shot 3] Close-up of Johnson and Marie drinking; Johnson is drinking faster and gets ready to pour another; Marie looks screen right.

[Shot 4] Long shot, Marie's point-of-view. Evidently she is looking at Morgan, who is center screen, looking in her direction (perhaps at Cricket).

[Shot 5] Mid-shot (almost a close-up) of Marie and Johnson, favoring Marie. She turns to look at Cricket, and the camera moves with her gaze. Cricket (in mid-shot) finishes the opening lines of the song: "Am I blue? Am I blue? Ain't these tears in my eyes telling you?" (The first "Am I blue" was sung in shot 3; the second begins in shot 4 and continues into shot 5; this subtly motivates our sense that Marie identifies with the persona of the song.)

[Shot 6] Close-up of Cricket at the piano, singing the next three lines of the song: "Am I blue? You'd be, too, If each plan with your man done fell—"

[Shot 7] "—through." Close-up of drummer, who folds up his newspaper and starts brushing the drums. As Cricket sings ("Was

44

a time, I was his only one, but now I'm—") the camera pulls back to reveal the ensemble (in mid-shot).

[Shot 8] (figure 6) Long shot, Morgan's point-of-view, but closer-in than shot 2. Johnson at screen left; a diagonal line runs down from Johnson's head to Marie's head to Cricket's head, which is at center screen; the right side of the screen is taken up by the piano and various elements of the audience. Johnson puts his hand on Marie's arm; she turns to take it off, then gets up to walk to the piano. Cricket sings, "the sad and lonely one, So lonely. Was I gay? 'til—" (It becomes clear in this shot that Marie is driven to the piano to escape Johnson's attentions rather than by a need to hog the audience's interest; by the next shot it is clear that she decides to use her position at the piano to attract Morgan.) So far the sequence has lasted exactly one minute.

[Shot 9] Close-up, from over Cricket's shoulder, as Marie leans on the piano and glances to the side, apparently in Morgan's direction. Cricket finishes the first verse: "—today. Now he's gone and we're through, Am I blue?"

[Shot 10] (figure 7) Mid-shot, from over Marie's shoulder; the camera is at standing height. Cricket, without missing a beat, tells Marie, "Take over," and starts singing "Was a time—". She picks up the line, "I was his only one—". Cricket is struck by her deep voice[50] and mugs his appreciation, then sings, "But now I'm—." She sings, "The sad and lonely one," looking over her shoulder, pointedly in Morgan's direction.

[Shot 11] Close-up of Morgan at his table, as at the end of shot 1. Cricket sings, "So lonely. Was I gay?"

[Shot 12] Same set-up as shot 9. Marie: "Was I gay?" Cricket: "til today—" Marie: "til today—"

[Shot 13] Same set-up as shot 10. Cricket: "Now she's gone and we're through, Baby oh—" and then Marie and Cricket finish the song together: "Am I blue? Am I blue?" There is a cut just after the end of the last chord.

---

50. Contrary to a widespread story that her songs were dubbed by Andy Williams, Bacall implies in *Lauren Bacall by Myself* (p. 100) that she did her own singing. It is of course possible that she sang for the camera *and* that Williams's track is the one used in the film's soundtrack; Bacall does not address that question.

[Shot 14] Same set-up as shot 8. (By repeating these set-ups Hawks and his excellent editor, Christian Nyby, are giving the song a sense of visual completion, working their way back to the conventional dramatic space as well as establishing, through repetition, that Marie and Cricket are comfortable with each other; they also create a back-and-forth pattern that matches the interchanges and rhythm of the song itself as well as clarifies the relationships among the characters. This particular set-up signifies Morgan's point-of-view and—since it is closer-in than shot 2 and an echo of shot 8—his concentrating his attention on Marie.) Johnson gets up, then gestures to Marie that he's going to the men's room. Someone requests another song; the audience is clapping and talking throughout the shot, and calls of "Bravo!" are distinct. Cricket tells his group to start up the song, and begins to plink-plink his way in, as Marie walks back to her table.

[Shot 15] Mid-shot: Frenchy comes in, agitated; camera tracks with him through the crowd and dips down to sitting level (and close-up) as he sits down at Morgan's table; by now the composition is like that at the end of shot 1, but set off at a slight angle. Frenchy explains that he couldn't get in touch with the radicals to stop them from coming (basically as in Faulkner's script); Morgan says that's not his problem; Frenchy gets up and leaves, but the camera remains on Morgan, shifting slightly to put him center screen.

[Shot 16] Long shot, Morgan's point-of-view; same set-up as shots 8 and 14. Marie steals Johnson's wallet from the table and waves broadly to Cricket as she starts walking screen right.

[Shot 17] Mid-shot: Marie walks through the crowd, and the camera tracks with her. She makes a very brief glance, apparently in Morgan's direction.

[Shot 18] Close-up of Morgan at his table; he thinks, then gets up to follow Marie; the camera does a short pan and tilt to follow him, as he follows her up the staircase (in what is by now a long shot).

It would be possible to go through the entire film this way, but the point has, I hope, been demonstrated. A few more general

46

observations on the finished picture will be offered here, and beyond these the reader is referred to the Illustrations section with its captions on lighting and shot composition, as well as, naturally, to the film itself.

To Have and Have Not is a film that makes its audience happy. There is a completely satisfying balance between good and evil, fun and melodrama, light wit and tough words, healthy sexuality and clear politics, and even between impotence (Eddy, a double-crosser without a stinger) and the redeeming power of love (Eddy again). The acting ranges from nonacting (Hoagy Carmichael playing himself with such ease that he achieves the most realistic mimesis, entirely in tone with the clean rhythm of the whole film and its no-nonsense, almost stoical clarity) to overacting (Dan Seymour playing Captain Renard with far too much melodramatics and an unfortunate accent, clearly a creature of the movies rather than of life, redeeming his performance only marginally in the last reel), as the interaction between the director and his co-creators ranges from the spontaneous (taking advantage of the developing emotion between Bogart and Bacall, which was made simpler by the necessity—thanks to the government and to Faulkner's being only a few days ahead of shooting—to shoot the film in sequence) to the entirely controlled (the lighting, for instance).

The originality of the film has an equally wide range: although there is simply no other film quite like *To Have and Have Not*, none so diverse yet so single-minded, so apparently meandering yet on reflection so efficient, so rich yet so spare—on the other hand, it is hard to think of a film that appears at first so derivative, not just of Hawks's earlier films but of Warners' most recent love-and-politics-and-Bogart-in-a-cafe romantic hit, *Casablanca*. In fact, one of the unique aspects of *To Have and Have Not* is that it is so superficially similar to and so profoundly different from the earlier melodrama.

This raises two quick literary comparisons: as Robin Wood has demonstrated, the writer whose attitudes Hawks most closely shares is Conrad (the theme of surrounding darkness, the importance of personal and ethical integrity, "the assertion of basic human qualities of courage and endurance, the stoical insistence on innate human dignity"),[51] but there is also a close connection with Shakespeare (who stole most of his plots, whose seamless work was addressed to a witty and regular audience, who neatly balanced comedy and tragedy, and who appears—to great advantage—not to have taken his dramatic work [as opposed to his poems] too "seriously"). I think the clearest way to point out how little it matters that Hawks "stole" much of this film from *Casablanca* is to draw on another of Wood's allusions: "*Only Angels Have Wings* is no more an imitation of Ford's *Air Mail* (for instance) than *Hamlet* is an imitation of *The Spanish Tragedy*."[52] Of course *Casablanca* offered a way of resolving what became the main problem in the script—the change of Fascists—and that led quite naturally to the reconception of Harry Morgan in terms of *Casablanca*'s Rick. To imitate *Casablanca*, it should by now be more than obvious, was not at all Hawks's original intention.

A quick comparing of the two melodramas reveals a difference, not so much of quality as of tone. *Casablanca* is romantic, but *To Have and Have Not* is a romance. *Casablanca* is centrifugal and compelling, a real gut-wrencher and tearjerker full of gauze shots and "big scenes" such as the singing of the "Marseillaise" and the magnificent conclusion. *To Have and Have Not* is more disciplined, open-handed, airy, elegant, cool, straight. It is almost the difference between Greek and Latin, or between Chaplin and Keaton. Even the songs point to this categorical difference. The romantic beauty of Ingrid Bergman and her Bogart is dreamily focused and intensified in "As Time Goes By," one of the most irresistible pieces of nostalgia in all sound film. The lithe sexiness of Lauren Bacall and her Bogart is sharpened, highlighted, and directed into action by "Am I Blue" and "How Little We Know," which range from the breezy to the honky-tonk. Carmichael's songs comment on the action in a light manner rather than drench it in emotion—for instance, in the "story of the very unfortunate colored man who got arrested down in old Hong Kong: he got twenty years' privilege taken away from him when he kicked old Buddha's gong," an upbeat allusion to Morgan's risky involvement with "lo-

51. Wood, *Howard Hawks*, p. 23.
52. Wood, *Howard Hawks*, p. 12.

cal politics." So that even if these films deal with many of the same issues (love and political commitment in particular), *Casablanca* is heavy where *To Have and Have Not* is light. One leans toward overstatement and the other toward understatement, but both involve real danger, real action, real love, real friendship, and a current world war in which some of the actors were deeply involved—Marcel Dalio in particular.[53] My point is that preference for one film or the other is a matter of personal taste, and that both films are equally serious.

The same could hardly be said of the Warner Brothers publicity campaign for this picture. As has already been mentioned, those elements of the film that were given most emphasis were the macho ones: Hawks the sportsman, Bogart the tough guy, Bacall the blonde, Moran the blonde . . . It was in fact a publicity avalanche, most of it centered on Bacall. Warners' head of publicity, Charles Einfeld, sent the following memo to his staff, and it may serve as an indication of the tone of the campaign as well as of the studio's enthusiasm for the picture:

Polish up the picks, shovels and pans for the gold mine on the way in Howard Hawks' production of Ernest Hemingway's *To Have and Have Not*, which we sneaked last night and which is not only a second *Casablanca* but two and a half times what *Casablanca* was. Here is a story of adventure and basic sex appeal the likes of which we have not seen since *Morocco* and *Algiers*. Bogart terrific, never was seen like this before. Lauren Bacall, new find of ours playing opposite Bogart, distinct personality who positively will be star overnight. Nothing like Bacall has been seen on the screen since Garbo and Dietrich. This is one of the biggest and hottest attractions we have ever had. If this sounds like I'm overboard, well I am.[54]

Many of the early reviews of the picture reflect this campaign rather than a careful response to the picture; this may of course be an occupational hazard of reviewing, press kit in lap, but there is

---

53. Best remembered for the two great roles he played for Jean Renoir—Rosenthal in *Grand Illusion* and the Marquis de la Chesnaye in *Rules of the Game*—Dalio (Frenchy/Gerard) was the son of Rumanian Jews living in France. He was forced to flee France, and while he was playing minor roles in the United States his parents were killed in a concentration camp.

54. Bacall, *Lauren Bacall by Myself*, p. 107.

little evidence that *To Have and Have Not* received during its first release anything like the intelligent attention it should have. Most of the reviews are of Bacall rather than of the film; some of them praise her, while the others give the impression of resisting her as if she were a gag to help sell a weak picture. Almost all of them point out that the film has little or nothing to do with the novel, but appear not to be upset about that; most of them assume that the source of the story, of the character of Morgan, and of the political attitudes in the film was simply *Casablanca*. If the film was praised, it was as a fast, witty romance; these reviewers, in other words, played into Hawks's cagey self-description as a director who considered plot "an excuse for some good scenes," and assumed there was nothing else going on. *Time* (October 23, 1944) called it a "tinny romantic melodrama which millions of cinemaddicts have been waiting for ever since *Casablanca*." *New York Variety* (October 14, 1944) said it was "not up to Warner's melodramatic story standards," an obvious attempt to follow up *Casablanca's* "lucrative box-office," characterized by "nifty productional accoutrements" but a "too unsteady" story line. Louella Parsons thought it was "definitely swell entertainment" (*Los Angeles Examiner*, January 20, 1945). The *Chicago Daily Tribune* (March 1, 1945) singled out Carmichael as the best actor in the film. Bosley Crowther (*New York Times*, October 12, 1944) considered it an enjoyable remake of *Casablanca*. Manny Farber (*The New Republic*, October 23, 1944) praised the complexity of Morgan's character, Bogart as a "Hemingway hero," and the fact that some of the dialogue "sounds as if it could have been thought up by the characters"; on the whole, however, he considered the film "spiritless," "half-hearted and slight," with "no more structure or unified effect than a string of familiar but unrelated beads." The *Daily Variety* (October 11, 1944) said the film "fails to materialize as any more than average, somewhat measuredly-paced melodrama where exciting action was rightfully anticipated" and felt Hawks "was handicapped by [a] meandering screenplay," which it called "too leisurely" and "entirely undistinctive." Other reviewers felt the movie's patriotism was too half-hearted, that Morgan was just out for himself. James Agee (*The Nation*, November 4, 1944) enjoyed it but thought *Going My Way* was better; he said, "It gets along on a mere thin excuse for a story, takes its time without trying to brag about its budget or to reel up footage for footage's sake, is an unusually happy exhibition of teamwork, and concentrates on character and atmosphere rather than plot. The best of the picture has no plot at all, but is a leisurely series of mating duels between Humphrey Bogart at his most proficient and the very entertaining, nervy, adolescent new blonde, Lauren Bacall. Whether or not you like the film will depend I believe almost entirely on whether you like Miss Bacall. I am no judge. I can hardly look at her . . . without getting caught in a dilemma between a low whistle and a bellylaugh. It has been years since I have seen such amusing pseudo-toughness on the screen. . . . I enjoyed watching something that obviously involved relaxed, improvising fun for those who worked on it, instead of the customary tight-lipped and hammer-hearted professional anxiety." It should come as no surprise that Agee was the most sensitive and articulate film critic of his time, but in this case even he could have done better.

The film went on to become one of the thirty top-grossing pictures of 1944. It received an award from the National Board of Review (and an export license!), but not even a nomination for an Academy Award. It was the year of *Going My Way, Double Indemnity, Laura, Gaslight, Since You Went Away, Meet Me in St. Louis, Lifeboat, The Uninvited, Thirty Seconds over Tokyo, Mr. Skeffington, Lady in the Dark,* and *Wilson.*

The first critics to pay serious attention to Hawks and to this film were those at *Cahiers*—most notably Godard, whose 1952 critique is the first to put the film in its proper rank and the only one I have seen that mentions Hawks's "increasingly precise taste for analysis" and his attempt to fix the "basic laws" of cinema "through a more rigorous knowledge of its limits." Not very much has been written about *To Have and Have Not* since then, except in the context of larger studies of Hawks.

The best of these one-man studies, in my judgment, is Robin Wood's, and some of his comments on the film deserve mention here. He does a good job on the "I like you and I don't like them" theme, for instance:

Hawks and Bogart give us a man who exists exclusively from his own centre, his actions stemming from the immediate perceptions and impulses of his consciousness. Here the term "individual" really means something: not merely "Someone who is different from other people," but "a conscious being who lives from his own feeling centre of identity." It is not a question of egotism: Morgan is never self-indulgent, or self-seeking beyond what he defines as his rights. He is a man whose sense of essential responsibility has been remarkably uncorrupted by either materialism or idealism.[55]

Calling it "one of the most basic anti-Fascist statements the cinema has given us," Wood recognizes in *To Have and Have Not* "all of Hawks's belief in the individual need for integrity and self-respect." He finds the film's "flexible and empirical morality" (Johnson's thieving is worse than Marie's, etc.) to be founded on the solid ground of Morgan's character, and calls Bogart's Morgan "the most perfect embodiment of the Hawks hero."

Hawks used to say that his first response to any new property was to try to make it into a comedy, and that only if that turned out to be absolutely impossible would he get serious. One of the interesting things about the making of *To Have and Have Not* is that although Hawks did succeed in turning Hemingway's pessimistic novel into a comedy (in the sense that from the outset it was intended that the story end on the note of Marie's and Morgan's impending marriage), he actually began with a series of scripts that were much more violent, negative, and dark than the final product. The story's lighter elements discovered themselves as Hawks and his collaborators worked along.

It is also ironic that *To Have and Have Not* should have emerged as so clearly "a Hawks film" when so many different people took a hand in its creation, some of them well outside Hawks's sphere of control. As a footnote to twentieth-century literature this film is even more of a paradox—or if you prefer, a red herring: Hemingway and Faulkner (with significant contributions from Furthman and Bogart) yield virtually pure Hawks. Still, "no man alone" could have created it. The film both addresses (via its story) and manifests (as a graceful collaboration) the importance of team-

55. Wood, *Howard Hawks*, p. 27.

work, of community. It is anti-Fascist not just in its theme of individualism but, more importantly, in this achieved sense of people's enjoying each other and working together well. Hawks is not the author but the auteur, the crest of the creative wave.

Hawks said he liked everything Hemingway wrote, and once even bought the rights to *The Sun Also Rises*, but sold them when he realized the censorship problems would be insurmountable. He had much the same reaction to Faulkner's *Sanctuary*, except that he didn't buy the rights. (One can only imagine what he might have done with a novel he did not consider Hemingway's worst.) In *To Have and Have Not* he managed in his characteristically cagey and subtle way to get his two hunting companions, Hemingway and Faulkner, to meet, although not in person and in such Hawksian terms that the casual viewer of the film would hardly recognize any trace of the two great novelists. Despite all the reverses and reconsiderations that went into it, then—the professional rivalries, the governmental interference, the pressures of time and money and love and war—*To Have and Have Not*, incredibly enough, fulfilled its original project: "You've got the character of Harry Morgan. I think I can give you the wife."

I am grateful to the people who helped me in the course of this project: the late Howard Hawks, Jorjana Kellaway, James Powers, Carole Raphalian, Anne Schlosser, Meta Carpenter Wilde, and Holly Yasui.

To Have And Have Not *(1944)*
U ● 1pm, TCM ★★★★★.

Lauren Bacall's dame in distress teaches Humphrey Bogart to whistle in Howard Hawks's sexy noir thriller. The Casablanca-style plot hasn't got a lot to do with Ernest Hemingway's source novel, but, frankly, with Bogie and Bacall's off-screen romance adding extra sizzle, who cares?

1. *Harry Morgan (Humphrey Bogart) examines the bottle of rum he found on Eddy. A poster of Pétain (the only prominent one in the film) hangs behind him.*

2. *Johnson (Walter Sande) gets his first strike as Morgan and Horatio (Sir Lancelot) watch. An example of Hawks's dynamic yet classically balanced composition—and the only scene in the film that appears in the novel.*

3. *Downtown Martinique. A Vichy agent approaches Morgan and Johnson from behind. These excellent sets have some of the flavor of Havana.*

4. *Morgan takes Frenchy/Gerard (Marcel Dalio) up to his room as Marie (Lauren Bacall) leaves hers. Faulkner's decision to have these rooms face each other facilitated their encounters and simplified the script.*

5. *"Anybody got a match?" asks Marie; Morgan throws her a box.*

6. *Johnson reaches for Marie as Cricket (Hoagy Carmichael) sings "Am I Blue" in the cafe of the Marquis Hotel.*

7. *Cricket reacts in mid-note to Marie's husky singing voice.*

8. *Eddy (Walter Brennan) explains to Beauclerc how drinking doesn't bother his memory. "If it did, I'd forget how good it was. Then where'd I be?" Morgan laughs affectionately in the background.*

9. *Sound/image rhythm: Marie stops Morgan from losing his temper by striking a match at the instant Morgan says, "and the bank opens at ten."*

10. *Frenchy, Morgan, and Marie size up the "Gestapo." A classical composition emphasizing Morgan's strength and centrality.*

11. *Marie tells the police she got off in Martinique "to buy a new hat" and gets slapped. Note the rich use of low-key lighting and composition in depth.*

12. *"The other times, you're just a stinker," says Marie, just before she kisses Morgan for the second time (and he "helps").*

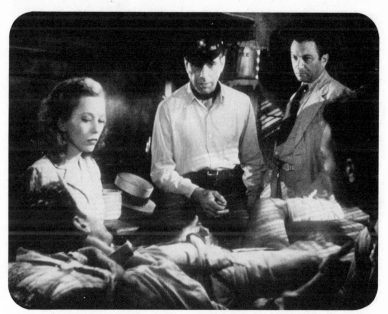

13. *Beauclerc (Paul Marion) tells Morgan how to pick up Paul de Bursac. As in figure 4, windowblind-light contributes greatly to the sense of place.*

14. *Eddy realizes that the reason Morgan didn't want to carry him on the "job" was to protect him. The night-sea fog motivates a rich range of grays.*

15. *Dolores Moran as Helene de Bursac. Morgan, who is in the middle of asking why anyone brought "a dame" along, is stopped by this smile.*

16. *Another remarkable integration of composition, lighting, and set design. Frenchy has just taken Morgan down to the cellar to tend Paul's wound; they are met by Helene, who will try to stop them.*

17. *Renard (Dan Seymour) tries to get Eddy drunk but gets a fish story for his pains.*

18. *In the cellar, Paul (Walter Molnar) explains his mission.*

19. *"How long will it take you to pack?" says Morgan, and Marie moves to kiss him.*

20. *Renard enters Morgan's room for the final interrogation.*

21. *Morgan shoots Renard's bodyguard (Aldo Nadi) through the drawer of the table.*

22. *Marie goes through the "dead bee" routine, and Eddy gets the feeling he's talking to himself.*

65

23. *Marie shimmies up to Morgan, and they leave the cafe.*

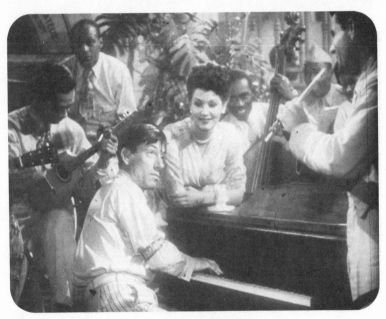

24. *Cricket signals for the last note, ending the film.*

To Have and Have Not

Screenplay

by

JULES FURTHMAN

and

WILLIAM FAULKNER

Based on the novel by

ERNEST HEMINGWAY

To Have and Have Not

Foreword

It is in Fort de France, the metropolis of Martinique, in the French West Indies, a few months after the signing of the Armistice between France and Germany.[1]

FADE IN

1. FORT DE FRANCE DOCK CLOSE SHOT EARLY MORNING [Large poster of Marshal Pétain on side of military hut. Somebody has neatly torn a large V out of it. CAMERA, DRAWING BACK, shows Chef de Poste, a quartermaster in the uniform of the French navy, dozing in chair tipped back underneath poster. Two Negro urchins, passing by, see what has happened to poster and pause to remark upon it in their soft patois. The quartermaster sits up, turns to see what they are laughing at, and notes V torn out of poster in great consternation. Furiously bidding the two urchins to be gone, he rushes into hut, returns with a new poster. Tearing down the old one, he quickly replaces it with the new one, fastening it in place with thumbtacks. Stepping back to survey his handiwork, he sees—to his amazement—that a large V still appears dimly in poster. Bewilderedly, he examines surface of poster and becomes aware that it is unmarked. Puzzled, he removes poster and looks at back of it. The V has been painted on the back. Crumpling up the poster in horror and rage, he rushes into hut, returning this time with a large framed portrait of Marshal Pétain, which he hangs upon rusty nail to cover the place occupied by poster. As he steps back to look at it, Morgan enters from street.][2]

[QUARTERMASTER:
Good morning, Captain Morgan. What can I do for you today?

MORGAN:
Same thing you did yesterday.

QUARTERMASTER:
You and your client wish to make a temporary exit from the port?

MORGAN:
Any objection?

Quartermaster looks very thoughtful and dubious, goes into hut, opens window, clears throat importantly, prepares to fill out form.

QUARTERMASTER:
Name?

MORGAN (patiently):
Harry Morgan.

QUARTERMASTER:
Nationality?

MORGAN:
American.

QUARTERMASTER:
Name of ship?

MORGAN:
Queen Conch, Key West, Florida.

QUARTERMASTER:
Purpose of excursion?

MORGAN:
Game fishing.

QUARTERMASTER:
Period of sojourn?

MORGAN:
We'll be back tonight.

QUARTERMASTER:
Length of trip?

MORGAN:
I don't think we'll go more than thirty miles off shore.

Quartermaster, writing this into form, signs it with a flourish, stamps it, and holds it out to Morgan.

QUARTERMASTER:
Five francs, please. (As Morgan pays money.) One thing more. You must return by sunset.

MORGAN (surprised):
Is that a new order?

QUARTERMASTER:
Yes. The decree was issued last night by His Excellency, Admiral Robert, governor general of the French West Indies. (Sharply.) Any complaints?

Morgan shakes head, raises hand holding pass in Nazi salute to portrait of Pétain.

MORGAN:
Vive l'empereur!

Then, as he walks out on dock, rusty nail gives way and portrait falls to ground. Quartermaster hurries out in alarm. As he starts to pick up picture, he sees a large cross of Lorraine (the de Gaulle emblem) painted on the back.][3]

2.   FORT DE FRANCE   DOCK
The *Queen Conch*, of Key West, Florida, a thirty-eight-foot fishing cruiser, is moored to the dock. The harbor in the background is alive with early morning traffic. Morgan enters on the dock [and sees that the Queen Conch has

slipped her stern line and is swinging, well away from the dock, by her bow line. Eddy is asleep in the fishing chair, one leg up over the stern. Morgan jumps down on the deck and goes down toward Eddy. He sees half a dozen empty beer bottles lying nearby. Eddy clutches another empty one to his chest. Morgan pulls the ship into the dock and secures the stern line properly. Then, he lifts Eddy by the scruff of the neck, lowers him over the side, dunks him briefly, and then sits him in the fishing chair again.

EDDY (grinning as he blinks water out of his eyes):
Hello, Harry. How's everything?

MORGAN:
Fine. Do you know the ship almost drifted away?

EDDY (looking around):
No, it never, Harry. All the lines are fast.

MORGAN:
They are now.

He goes amidships and Eddy follows him.

EDDY:
Where you been, Harry? Did you bring me a drink?

Morgan lifts the lid of the icebox, sees all the beer gone but one bottle. He picks that up, opens it. Eddy beams, reaches for it.

EDDY:
I was saving that.

MORGAN:
For me? (Puts bottle to his lips.) Thanks.

Eddy's face falls, and he watches Morgan with thirsty absorption. Morgan looks at him standing there, tall and hollow cheeked, with his mouth loose and that white stuff in the corners of his eyes and his scant hair all faded from the sun. Morgan knows he is dead for a drink.

MORGAN (handing him the bottle):
  Here.

EDDY (beaming again):
  Harry, you're my pal. I sure got them this morning.

MORGAN:
  You have them every morning.

EDDY (draining bottle):
  You're sure swell, Harry. Sometimes I wonder why you're so good to me.

MORGAN:
  I wonder all the time. (Nodding toward dock.) Give Horatio a hand.]⁴

Horatio, the Negro bait cutter, enters on dock carrying a case of beer on his head. Horatio is a real black Martinique Negro, smart and gloomy, with blue voodoo beads around his neck under his shirt and an old straw hat, which he now carries in his hand. What he likes to do ashore at night is to rhumba, and aboard ship he likes to sleep and read the papers. Aided by Eddy, he comes aboard and rests the case of beer on the side of the icebox.

[HORATIO:
  Good morning, Captain. That chef de hoste took a bottle of our beer.]⁵

MORGAN:
  That's all right, Mr. Johnson can afford it.

[EDDY (looking at the sun):
  He's almost an hour late, Harry. Maybe he isn't going out today.

MORGAN:
  He'll be here.

HORATIO (looking toward street):
  Here he comes now.

Johnson enters on the dock. Johnson is a plump, pursy-faced businessman of forty-five, clad in the sporting-goods-store conception of a practical fishing costume for the tropics: pith helmet, etc.

EDDY:
Good morning, Mr. Johnson. How's everything?

Johnson nods sourly. It is evident he doesn't think much of Eddy.

JOHNSON (jumping down on deck):
Morning. (To Morgan.) Well, are we going out?

MORGAN:
That's up to you, Mr. Johnson.

JOHNSON (looking at the sky):
What sort of a day will it be?

MORGAN:
Just about like yesterday. Maybe better.][6]

JOHNSON (lighting a cigar):
Let's go out then.

MORGAN (to Horatio):
Cast off those lines.

HORATIO:
All right, Captain.

Eddy goes astern and starts throwing empty beer bottles over the side.

MORGAN:
I've got to put some gas in her, Mr. Johnson.

JOHNSON:
All right.

MORGAN (starting motors):
[I'll need some money for that.][7]

JOHNSON (taking out wallet):
How much?

MORGAN:
It's twenty-eight cents a gallon. I ought to put in forty
gallons anyway. That's eleven dollars and twenty
cents.

JOHNSON (taking some bills out of wallet):
Here's fifteen dollars.

MORGAN (taking money):
I'll get change for you at the gas dock.

JOHNSON:
Never mind. Just put it down against what I owe
you.

He goes astern and sits down in fishing chair. Horatio
casts off stern line and jumps aboard. As Morgan takes
ship away from the dock and heads out into the stream,

FADE OUT

FADE IN

3.   EXT. OCEAN NEAR MARTINIQUE COASTLINE   LATER THAT DAY
Big marlin leaping out of water and making vain attempt
to free itself from hook.

4.   EXT. MORGAN'S FISHING BOAT NEARBY
Johnson in stern holding rod. Horatio, the Negro bait cutter, folds up newspaper and sits up to watch. Eddy, the
rummy, is sleeping on deck. Harry Morgan at wheel yells:

[MORGAN:
Sock him again. Stick it into him. Hit him three-four
times—][8]

Johnson obeys and hits fish pretty hard a couple of times
more. Then the rod bends double, the reel screeches, and
out jumps the marlin—boom—in a long straight jump,
shining silver in the sun and making a splash like throwing a horse off a cliff.

JOHNSON:
  I've got him—

MORGAN:
  Ease up on the drag.

JOHNSON (as line goes slack):
  He's gone—

[MORGAN:
  No, he's not. Ease up on the drag quick— (To Horatio.) Get those teasers in—

Horatio goes and pulls in teasers, while the fish jumps again and heads out to sea.

JOHNSON (as line slacks again):
  He's gone—

Morgan shakes his head.

MORGAN (spinning wheel to follow fish):
  Reel in on him. He's hooked good—][9]

HORATIO:
  He sure is.

Then once, twice, the big fish comes out stiff as a post, the whole length of him jumping toward the boat, throwing the water high each time he lands.

[JOHNSON (as line slacks once more):
  He's gone.

MORGAN:
  I'll tell you when he's gone. Reel in fast and keep the drag light—][10]

Johnson (all thumbs) works at reel and all of a sudden his rod jerks and the line goes slack.

MORGAN (in disgust):
  Well, he's gone now—

HORATIO:
> Yes, sir—he's gone now.

JOHNSON:
> No, he's not—turn around and chase him—

But Morgan merely stares after marlin, which is still jumping and keeps on jumping until he is out of sight.

MORGAN:
> Reel in your line—

JOHNSON:
> I tell you I can still feel him pull—

MORGAN (leaving the wheel):
> That's the weight of the line—

JOHNSON:
> You're crazy. I can hardly reel it. Maybe he's dead—

MORGAN:
> Maybe—but he's still jumping.

[He feels the drag. Johnson has screwed it down tight. You couldn't pull out any line. It had to break.

MORGAN (angrily):
> Didn't I tell you to keep your drag light?

JOHNSON:
> But he kept taking out line.

MORGAN:
> So what?

JOHNSON:
> So I tightened the drag.

MORGAN (patiently):
> Listen, if you don't give them line when they hook up like that, they break it.

JOHNSON:
> Then you ought to get stronger line—

MORGAN:

> There isn't any line will hold them. When they want it, you've got to give it to them. And you have to keep the drag light as a feather—

JOHNSON:

> I know—I know—you don't have to rub it in—][11] (To Horatio, the Negro bait cutter, who is fixing up a couple of fresh mackerel.) Come on, you—hurry up.

HORATIO (cheerfully):

> I'm hurrying, Mr. Johnson.

He deftly passes the hook through the mouth of the mackerel, out the gills, slitting the side and then putting the hook through the other side and out, tying the mouth shut on the wire leader and tying the hook good so it can't slip and so the bait will troll smooth without spinning.

JOHNSON (to Morgan):

> Can't you put on a bait like that, captain?

MORGAN:

> Yes—sure I can.

JOHNSON:

> Then why do you carry this fellow to do it?

MORGAN:

> When the big fish run you'll see why.

JOHNSON:

> What's the idea?

MORGAN:

> Horatio can do it faster than I can.

[JOHNSON (nodding toward the sleeping Eddy):

> Can't Eddy do it?

MORGAN:

> No, he can't.

JOHNSON:
> A dollar a day. It seems an unnecessary expense to me.

MORGAN:
> He's necessary—aren't you, Horatio?

HORATIO:
> I hope so.

Eddy wakes up, comes back astern.

EDDY:
> ` What's the matter?

Morgan knows he woke up dead for a drink.

MORGAN:
> You'd better drink a bottle of beer.][12]

Eddy goes to the icebox.

JOHNSON (sourly, reeling in line):
> I don't see why you want that rummy around for.

MORGAN:
> Eddy was a good man on a boat once, before he got to be a rummy.

JOHNSON:
> Well, he isn't any good now. Is he related to you or something?

MORGAN:
> Nope.

JOHNSON:
> Then why d'you look after him?

Morgan looks out toward Eddy and grins.

MORGAN:
> He thinks he's looking after me.

Eddy comes astern, polishing off bottle of beer with deep relish.

EDDY:
>Mr. Johnson, d'you care if I ask you a question?

He tosses empty bottle into sea, and Johnson sourly looks after it.

JOHNSON:
>Listen, mister, it might interest you to know that I not only paid for that beer, but I also put a deposit on the bottles.

EDDY:
>Was you ever bit by a dead bee?

JOHNSON:
>A dead what?

EDDY:
>A dead honeybee?

[JOHNSON (turning his back):
>I never was bit by any kind of a bee.][13]

EDDY (winking at Morgan):
>Well, in that case, I'll just finish my nap. Thanks for the beer, Mr. Johnson.

As Johnson turns to glare at him, Horatio lets out a warning yip and Morgan yells at Johnson.

MORGAN:
>Watch your line!

Johnson turns and sees a big marlin burst head and shoulders out of the water and smash at mackerel with his sword.

[MORGAN (returning to wheel):
>Slack it to him—

JOHNSON:
He hasn't got it—

MORGAN:
Yes, he has. And he's a big one. I'll bet he'll go a thousand pounds—

JOHNSON:
I tell you he hasn't got it—][14]

In reply, the marlin jumps straight up beside the boat, and Johnson rises up in his chair as though he was being derricked, and he stands there clinging to the rod for a second and the rod bending like a bow, and then the butt catches him in the belly and the whole works goes overboard, rod, reel, tackle, and all.

MORGAN (shutting off engine):
Well, I guess that's enough for one day—

Johnson sits down, holding onto his belly where the rod butt had hit him.

JOHNSON (dazedly):
What happened?

MORGAN:
[Nothing. You just had the drag screwed down tight again, that's all, and when the fish struck, it just naturally lifted you right out of your chair and you couldn't hold it.

HORATIO (chuckling):
You had the harness on, that fish'd've taken you along with him.

EDDY (slapping Johnson on the back):
Mr. Johnson, you're just unlucky. Now, maybe you're lucky with women. Mr. Johnson, what d'you say we go out tonight?][15]

JOHNSON (rising enragedly and hitting Eddy in the face):
I'll lucky you, you dirty rummy—

MORGAN (grabbing him as he makes a rush toward Eddy):
Mr. Johnson, are you a good swimmer?

JOHNSON (struggling to get at Eddy):
I've stood all I'm going to—

MORGAN:
So have I—so be careful you don't slip out of my hand.

EDDY (interposing):
Take it easy, Harry—that guy owes you for sixteen days.

[JOHNSON:
Fifteen!][16]

DISSOLVE TO:

5.   EXT. MARTINIQUE DOCK   SUNSET
[Quartermaster dozing in chair tipped back under portrait of Pétain. Morgan, coming up from dock with Johnson, stops and leaves pass in quartermaster's lap. Johnson does the same. As they start on, Johnson indicates tricolor hanging from mast on quartermaster's hut.

JOHNSON:
I thought everybody took down their flag after sunset.

MORGAN:
Most people do.][17]

JOHNSON:
That's Vichy for you.

MORGAN (indifferently):
It's their flag.

[A slit-eyed civilian, leaning against kiosk, lowers newspaper and looks after them.][18]

6.   EXT. FORT DE FRANCE   WATERFRONT STREET
Morgan enters with Johnson. Negro beggar drinking out

of fountain. Slit-eyed civilian, entering and hurrying after them, lifts his hat and speaks to them.

CIVILIAN:
Pardon me, gentlemen.

Morgan and Johnson stop.

CIVILIAN (taking out notebook):
May I have your names?

MORGAN:
What for?

CIVILIAN:
I heard this gentleman make a disparaging reference to Vichy.

He nods toward Johnson.

JOHNSON:
Me? I never said a word about Vichy. (To Morgan.) Did I?

MORGAN:
I wasn't paying much attention.

[JOHNSON:
I was just talking about the attitude of the American government. I said it was very wishy-washy.

CIVILIAN:
You are both Americans?

JOHNSON:
Yes.

CIVILIAN (raising hat):
Pardon me. I thought you were English.][19]

He turns and leaves. Morgan and Johnson continue down the street toward entrance of combination cafe and hotel.

7.   INT. CAFE
Morgan and Johnson enter and pause at bar, behind
which hangs usual large portrait of Pétain. At the piano
in far corner sits Cricket, the piano player, working on
song. Two waiters on. Gerard, the French proprietor, is
checking cash register behind bar, and as Morgan and
Johnson give order to bartender:

[GERARD:
Well, gentlemen—what luck today? (To bartender.)
That's Captain Morgan's bottle. How many times do
I have to tell you?][20]

MORGAN:
Not so good, Frenchy.

JOHNSON:
We lost the biggest fish I ever saw.

GERARD (in sympathy):
Well, maybe tomorrow you hook him again.

[JOHNSON:
I give up. I'm through. I'm fed up with this kind of
fishing.

MORGAN:
I don't blame you. You fish for sixteen days, hook
into a couple of fish any good fisherman would give
a year to tie into—

JOHNSON:
All right—all right. Don't rub it in. (Taking out wallet.) I haven't got enough here to pay you off. I'll go
to the bank in the morning.

MORGAN:
Okay. (Finishes drink.) See you later.

He starts toward rear. Gerard follows him, overtaking
him as he ascends stairway, which leads toward landing,
thence into hotel section.

GERARD:

> Harry, there were some people asking for you to-
> day.][21]

MORGAN (pausing):
> Fishermen?

GERARD:

> No. Some friends of— (looking around cautiously) of
> friends of mine.

[Morgan looks at him, smiles shrewdly, and shakes his
head. Gerard takes his arm and starts down hallway in
hotel section.

8.   INT. HALLWAY HOTEL SECTION
Gerard walking with Morgan.

GERARD:

> They only want to use your ship for one night. They
> will pay you very well, too. Of course, nothing like
> you would get from Americans.

MORGAN (shaking head):
> I'd like to oblige you, Frenchy, but I can't afford to
> get mixed up in local politics.

GERARD:

> It is a very urgent matter. Afterwards, when things
> are different, it would be very good for you, Harry.][22]

As Morgan stops by door of room and starts to unlock it,
the door on opposite side of hall is opened, and Marie
comes out with unlighted cigarette in her hand.

[MARIE (seeing Gerard):
> Have you got a match?

Gerard searches his pockets and turns to Morgan, who
has been doing the same.

MORGAN (opening door):
I think I've got some in here.

He goes in, followed by Gerard.

9.　INT. MORGAN'S SITTING ROOM
Morgan enters, followed by Gerard. Marie pauses in doorway, looking into room. Morgan, opening drawer of table, looks at her as he takes out box of matches. He has placed her in this gaze, and his next movement confirms it.

MORGAN (tossing box to Marie):
Here you are.][23]

She catches it, extracts a match, lights cigarette, then, closing box, she tosses it back to him.

MARIE:
Thanks.

Closing door, she exits.

[MORGAN:
When did she get in?

GERARD:
This afternoon.

MORGAN:
On the plane from the south? (As Gerard nods.) What's her racket?

GERARD:
What makes you think she has one?

Morgan shrugs, and pushes up the transom.

MORGAN:
Look, Frenchy. About this other thing. The Vichy crowd is on top here and if they catch me fooling around with the de Gaullist bunch, I'll be cooked. Probably lose my ship to boot.

GERARD (resignedly):
> You know best, Harry.

MORGAN:
> I'm all for you, Frenchy—you know that.

GERARD:
> Let's have dinner together.

He opens door to leave.

MORGAN (starting to remove shirt):
> Soon as I have a shower.][24]

FADE OUT

FADE IN

10. INT. CAFE THAT NIGHT

[Intimate group around piano, where Cricket is playing some nostalgic song. Marie, sitting at nearby table with Johnson, is singing. They have just finished dinner, and it is evident Johnson is making a play for her. Morgan, dining with Gerard at table across the room, is studying Marie.][25] A colored boy enters and whispers something to Gerard. Latter, dismissing boy, utters an exclamation of concern. Morgan turns and looks at him.

GERARD:
> I tried to head those fellows off, but I can't get in contact with them.

MORGAN (looking out at Marie again):
> The ones that wanted to hire my ship?

GERARD:
> It is dangerous enough for them to come here at all— but to come here for nothing—

Morgan is watching Marie as she finishes song.

[MORGAN:
> Why don't you go outside and keep an eye open for them?

GERARD (nodding toward Marie):
    You like her voice?

MORGAN:
    Not bad.

Gerard finishes his coffee, rises, and goes out toward rear. As he exits, Morgan sees Johnson excuse himself to Marie and start unsteadily across floor toward men's room in hallway behind her. As he exits, Marie finishes brandy, picks up bag, and starts toward stairway in rear. Morgan watches her as she approaches. She sees him, and as she passes she says pleasantly:

MARIE:
    Good evening.

MORGAN (same tone):
    How are you?][26]

Marie looks at him over shoulder as she ascends stairway, and Morgan, finishing his coffee, rises and follows her.

11.   INT. HALLWAY   HOTEL SECTION
Marie enters and comes down hall, taking key out of bag. Morgan enters, and Marie sees him as she pauses to unlock door. He walks up to her and holds out his hand.

[MORGAN:
    Let's have it, Slim.

MARIE:
    What do you want?

MORGAN:
    Johnson's wallet.

MARIE:
    Are you drunk?

In reply he takes her by the arm, leads her across hall, opens door of his room, and shoves her inside.

12.   INT. MORGAN'S SITTING ROOM
Morgan, entering with Marie, closes door.

MARIE:
Say, mister, what's got into you?

MORGAN (holding out hand):
Come on, Slim.

MARIE:
Listen—nobody calls me Slim. I'm too skinny to take it kindly.

MORGAN:
All right—if you want it that way.

He starts toward her; Marie backs away from him.

MARIE:
What are you going to do?

MORGAN:
Quit that baby talk.

Marie stares at him for a moment, then smiles.

MARIE:
You know, Steve—I wouldn't put it past you.

She takes wallet out of bosom of dress and looks at Morgan.

MARIE:
I thought you were a fisherman—not a hotel detective.][27]

MORGAN:
Johnson's my client.

MARIE:
He doesn't speak so well of you.

[MORGAN:
He's still my client. Another thing, I don't care for small crooks.

MARIE:
> I didn't take it from him. He dropped it and I picked it up.][28]

MORGAN:
> Oh, you were going to give it back to him?

MARIE:
> No, I wasn't. I don't like him.

MORGAN:
> That's a good reason.

[MARIE:
> Besides, I've got to have some money to get out of here.

MORGAN:
> That's another good reason—but you'll have to pick on somebody else.][29]

Morgan takes wallet out of her hand, opens it on table and examines contents.

MORGAN (in disgust):
> Humph! How d'you like that? [Sixty dollars in cash and fourteen hundred dollars in traveler's checks!

MARIE:
> I'll settle for the sixty bucks.

MORGAN:
> That bird owes me eight hundred and twenty-five. "I haven't got that much on me," he says. "I'll go to the bank and pay you off tomorrow," he says. (Looking at airline ticket.) And all the time he's got this reservation in his kick for a plane that leaves here at daylight.

MARIE:
> He was going to slip out on you?][30]

MORGAN (nodding):
Good thing you didn't give it back to him.

MARIE:
Then I did you a favor?

[MORGAN:
Sure did. (Picks up one of the bills.) Here.

Marie takes bill and looks at it.

MARIE (as if amazed at his generosity):
Twenty dollars!

MORGAN:
You can use it, can't you?

MARIE:
Sure I could. But I wouldn't dream of taking it. I couldn't. I only saved you eight hundred and twenty-five.

Morgan, staring at her, snatches the bill out of her hand.

MORGAN:
You saved it for me?

MARIE:
Well, you'd never known Johnson was going if it hadn't been for me, would you?

Morgan stares at her for a moment, then grins, starting to replace bills and things in wallet.

MORGAN:
That's right. What d'you think is fair?

MARIE:
I'll leave it to you.

MORGAN:
What d'you say to fifty-fifty?

MARIE (startled):
Fifty-fifty?

MORGAN:

Sure. If I hadn't stopped you, you'd have got away with the whole works, wouldn't you? After all, I'm entitled to something.

Marie grins.

MARIE:

Forget it. If I don't owe *you* anything I'm satisfied.

She starts toward door, but pauses as somebody knocks.

MORGAN:

Who is it?][31]

Door is opened, and Gerard enters with three young Frenchmen in civilian clothes.

[GERARD:

Harry, these are friends of mine who wanted to charter your boat.

Marie starts toward door again.

MARIE:

See you later.

MORGAN:

Sit down. We're not through yet. (To Gerard.) I told you I wasn't interested.

GERARD:

That's what I told them—but Beauclerc wants to talk to you.

MORGAN:

You fellows better clear out of here.

BEAUCLERC:

We're not afraid.

MORGAN:

Well, I am.

Beauclerc shrugs resignedly and turns to one of the others.

BEAUCLERC:
Go and see if the street is clear.

GERARD:
I'll go.

He exits and the three young Frenchmen stand there looking sad.

MORGAN:
I'm sorry, boys—but I can't do it.][32]

BEAUCLERC:
We will give you twenty-five hundred francs.

MORGAN:
That's fifty dollars in American money. [I can't do it.

DE GAULLIST NO. 1:
A thousand francs a piece. (Morgan shakes his head.) It is only a little voyage to a place about forty kilometers from here.][33]

BEAUCLERC:
We would give you more money—but we haven't got it.

[MORGAN:
Don't make me feel bad. I tell you true I can't do it.][34]

DE GAULLIST NO. 2:
Afterwards, when things are changed, it would mean a good deal to you.

[MORGAN:
I know. But I can't do it.

BEAUCLERC:
I thought all Americans were friendly to our side.

MORGAN:
> Look—they send you fellows to Devil's Island. I'm not that friendly to anybody.

BEAUCLERC:
> They wouldn't dare do that to an American.

MORGAN:
> They would if I was caught with you fellows.

There is a moment of silence. Beauclerc looks at Marie.

BEAUCLERC:
> Is she your sweetheart?

MORGAN:
> No.

Then the door opens and Eddy breezes in.][35]

EDDY (brightly):
> Hello, Harry—how you been keeping?

[BEAUCLERC (unbuttoning his coat):
> Who is he?

MORGAN:
> A friend of mine—

EDDY:
> How'd you come out with Mr. Johnson?

MORGAN:
> Fine. Who's looking after the ship?

EDDY (smiling):
> I am. But I got a little thirsty waiting by myself.

MORGAN:
> Go on back. There's a bottle in the tool chest.

EDDY:
> Thanks, Harry. You're a good boy. You're a credit to me. Who are these guys?

MORGAN:
I don't know.

EDDY (pointing to Beauclerc):
He was hanging around the dock for a while after you left—

BEAUCLERC:
You've got a good memory for a drunk—][36]

EDDY:
Drinking don't bother my memory. If it did I wouldn't drink. I couldn't. You see, I'd forget how good it was. Then where would I be? I'd start drinking water again.

BEAUCLERC:
Maybe you'd forget about water, too.

EDDY:
No, I wouldn't. I see too much of it. Was you ever bit by a dead bee?

The three young Frenchmen laugh.

BEAUCLERC (after a moment):
I have no memory of being bit by any kind of a bee—

MARIE: (to Eddy):
Were you?

Eddy beams at her in great delight.

EDDY:
Say, lady, you're all right. You and Harry are the only ones that ever—

MORGAN:
Don't forget Frenchy.

EDDY:
That's right. You and Harry and Frenchy. You've got to be careful of dead bees when you're going around barefooted. If you step on them they can sting you

just as bad as if they were alive. Especially if they
were kind of mad when they got killed. I bet I've
been bit a hundred times that way—

MARIE:
You have? Why don't you bite them back?

[EDDY (grinning at her):
That's what Harry always says. But I haven't got a
stinger—

DE GAULLIST NO. 1 (to Morgan):
Does he always talk so much?

MORGAN:
Always— (To Eddy.) I'll be down to the dock in a
little while—

EDDY:
Okay. So long.][37]

Eddy gives them a wave and exits.

[MORGAN:
Sorry, gentlemen. Where were we?

DE GAULLIST NO. 2:
You would have three thousand francs and it could
mean a great deal to you later. All this will not last,
you know.

BEAUCLERC:
If you take us on this small journey I can almost
promise it will not last.

MORGAN:
Listen, I don't care who runs France or Martinique.
Or who wants to. Please get somebody else. (To
Marie.) Come on—we've got some unfinished busi-
ness of our own.

Morgan nods to Marie and starts toward the door. Beauclerc bows courteously to Marie as she passes.

BEAUCLERC:
Good night.

MARIE:
Good night.][38]

Morgan opens door and they exit.

13.   HOTEL HALLWAY   OUTSIDE OF MORGAN'S ROOM
Morgan and Marie come out of his room.

[MARIE:
Do you have to take me along?

MORGAN:
Wouldn't you rather do your own lying?

MARIE:
Let's go.

They exit.][39]

14.   INT. THE CAFE
Morgan and Marie come down the steps and meet Johnson near the bar.

JOHNSON (to Marie):
Where have you been? I've been looking all over for
you. (To Morgan.) You're a fine one—running off
with my girl.

MORGAN:
She's got something she wants to tell you. (He leans
against the bar.) Go ahead, Slim.

MARIE (extending the wallet):
Here's your wallet.

JOHNSON (missing the wallet for the first time):
Where did you get it?

MARIE (with a look at Morgan):
    I stole it.

JOHNSON:
    Well—that's a fine thing. (He is a little confused.)
    What are you going to do about it?

MORGAN (who has been watching this):
    The question is, what are you going to do, Mr. John-
    son?

Johnson looks at Morgan, realizing for the first time that
maybe Morgan has examined the wallet.

MORGAN (continuing):
    Maybe you had better take a look and see if it's all
    there.

JOHNSON (stuttering):
    Oh, I'm sure it's—it's all right.

MORGAN:
    Check it over. She might want a receipt for it.

Johnson gives contents of wallet a hasty, perfunctory
glance.

JOHNSON:
    It's all right. Nothing missing.

MORGAN:
    You sure?

JOHNSON (trying to change the subject):
    Yes. Now, young lady, I don't—

MORGAN (interrupting):
    You had better count those traveler's checks.

[JOHNSON (reluctantly obeying):
    Fourteen hundred.][40]

MORGAN (getting quiet and taking out a cigarette):
    But you had to go to the bank tomorrow.

Johnson is scared.

MORGAN:
> What's the time on that plane ticket you've got there?
> (He is starting to move.)

JOHNSON:
> Six-thirty.

MORGAN (on the move):
> In the morning. And the bank opens at ten.

Just then, Marie strikes a match and holds it in front of Morgan and lights his cigarette. He pauses and after a moment grins at her.

MORGAN:
> I don't like him any better than you do.

JOHNSON:
> Look, Mr. Morgan. I was going to—

MORGAN (interrupting):
> Going to sign some of those checks, weren't you?

[JOHNSON:
> Why, surely. I—

MORGAN (to the bartender):
> Got a fountain pen?

As the bartender looks for the fountain pen, the three de Gaullists come down the stairs headed for the door.

MORGAN (waving to them):
> Good luck.][41]

Morgan hands the fountain pen to Johnson, and as the latter starts to sign the first of the checks, Morgan, glancing toward the front door, grabs Marie and shoves her out of the way.

15. INT. CAFE   SHOOTING TOWARD FRONT DOOR AND WINDOWS
Three young de Gaullists, standing on sidewalk, are
drawing revolvers and ducking behind ice wagon as big
sedan lurches by with a machine gun spitting fire through
open window in back. The staccato blast riddles cafe windows breast high on that side and smashes bottles all
along wall behind bar and knocks chips of ice out of ice
wagon. Beauclerc, climbing up on wheel of ice wagon,
fires over driver's seat at sedan.

16. EXT. STREET IN FRONT OF CAFE
Sedan, swinging sharply to right, jumps over curb,
crashes into colonnade, and stops in shop window. Two
big fellows crawl out of rear door. One has a Thompson
gun and the other has a sawed-off shotgun.
  The one with the machine gun is Captain Renard of the
Sûreté Nationale. The one with the sawed-off shotgun is
Lieutenant Coyo. Driver of ice wagon runs out of Cunard
Bar and goes to heads of plunging horses. Coyo knocks
him over with a blast from sawed-off shotgun. De Gaullist
No. 1 behind rear of ice wagon fires, and bullet ricochets
off street and hits rear tire of car. You can see dust blowing up from street as the air comes out. Renard gets down
almost on face and starts to fire a burst under ice wagon.

17. INT. CAFE
Morgan, on floor, is dragging Marie behind bar.

[MARIE (dazedly):
    Say, what on earth—?

MORGAN:
    Lie down.][42]

He puts both arms around her and holds her close to him
as bullets whiz behind to riddle cabinets and bar fixtures
just above their heads.

18.   EXT. STREET IN FRONT OF CAFE
        De Gaullist No. 2, shot, is lying on sidewalk behind ice
        wagon. De Gaullist No. 1 stoops to lift him up and is cut
        down himself. Beauclerc, standing on wheel and firing
        over driver's seat, sees this, grabs reins, and climbs inside
        wagon, driving horses down the street. Renard and Coyo
        run after wagon, firing into rear filled with ice. Chips fly
        and huge hunks fall out as horses break into a gallop and
        wagon lumbers around distant corner with Renard and
        Coyo following on foot.

19.   EXT. HAVANA SIDE STREET
        Ice wagon enters and Beauclerc pulls up horses by alley.
        He climbs out and dives down alley as Renard and Coyo
        run around corner, pausing cautiously as they see aban-
        doned ice wagon.

20.   INT. CAFE
        Gerard, who has been near the door watching what is
        going on in the street, comes running back to Morgan and
        Marie.

        [MORGAN:
            Did they get them all?

        GERARD (excitedly):
            One got away at least. I think it was Beauclerc. Look,
            Harry, this is bad. But no one but me knows that you
            two saw them. And Eddy.

        MORGAN:
            He probably won't remember.][43]

        GERARD (continuing):
            When the police come, you know nothing. (Turning
            to Marie.) Nothing. Do you realize, mademoiselle?

        MARIE:
            Yes.

[MORGAN:
    She won't talk.][44]

They are interrupted by the bartender's voice.

BARTENDER:
    Monsieur Gerard! Monsieur Gerard!

They turn and see the bartender bending over the body of Johnson. Morgan comes in and rolls him over. Johnson has been shot neatly through the head. Marie stares at Morgan. Morgan takes the traveler's checks and the wallet out of Johnson's hands. He removes the bank notes from the wallet, puts the checks into the wallet, and puts the wallet into Johnson's pocket and the money into his own pocket.

[MORGAN:
    He couldn't write any faster than he could duck. (Marie stares at him.) Too bad they couldn't have put off saving France for a while. Another minute and those checks would have been good.][45]

There is the sound of a police whistle, and they turn toward the door. A sergeant of the gendarmes comes in followed by half a dozen French sailors.

GENDARME:
    Keep quiet everyone. Stay right where you are.

(NOTE: Do this two ways, in English and in French.)

In the silence that follows, we see three menacing-looking men in plain clothes come quietly in, stopping in the center of the open space and looking over the people. They are Renard, Coyo, and Renard's bodyguard. At the bar, Morgan whispers to Gerard.

[MORGAN:
    Who are they?

GERARD (alarmed):
Sûreté Nationale.

MORGAN:
The Gestapo, huh?][46]

They look back at the men, who then start to move around staring at the faces.

RENARD (followed by his bodyguard; sees Johnson):
What happened to this man?

GERARD:
A stray bullet. His name is Johnson—an American.

RENARD (speaking quietly):
Unfortunate. (To a couple of sailors.) Take him away.

He leans against the bar and takes his time and speaks softly to the entire group.

[RENARD:
All this is regrettable. There is no cause for alarm. We are only interested in those persons who have broken the rules laid down for their behavior. I will pick out certain individuals. Those I do not designate will leave immediately. This place will then remain closed for tonight.][47]

Renard then commences walking, pointing out various people, among them Gerard, Morgan, Marie, etc. As Renard points to Marie and passes on, she whispers to Morgan.

MARIE:
Was you ever bit by a dead bee?

At this point, past the sailors guarding the door, we see Eddy sailing serenely in. Suddenly, he stops, takes note of the bristling military situation, turns around, and leaves with the same enthusiasm that brought him in.

FADE OUT

21.   INT. POLICE OFFICE   NIGHT

Morgan, Marie, and Gerard are being questioned. Renard sits behind the desk and the bodyguard stands beside him. Coyo questions Gerard first.

GERARD:
  I tell you again. I didn't know those men. They came in for a drink. That's all I know.

COYO:
  You never saw them before?

GERARD:
  No.

[COYO:
  That's all. You may go.][48]

As Gerard turns to exit, Renard speaks.

RENARD:
  What are your sympathies, Monsieur Gerard?

GERARD:
  I am for France.

RENARD:
  That is well. Try to remain so.

Gerard moves on again. As Renard speaks to Coyo, Gerard pauses to listen.

RENARD:
  Let us suggest to Monsieur Gerard that the next time suspicious characters enter his place that he notify us. By that means, he may prevent bloodshed at his doorstep.

GERARD:
  I run a public place. How am I to know who is suspicious and who is not?

RENARD:
  I think you will know. Good night.

[Gerard exits. Renard speaks to Coyo.

RENARD (to Coyo):
Continue.][49]

COYO (to Morgan):
And you did not see these men at all while they were in the cafe?

MORGAN:
That's right.

COYO:
What was your connection with the dead man?

MORGAN:
He rented my boat to fish from.

COYO:
You mean he had rented it. According to this ticket in his wallet, he was to have left Martinique at day-light.

RENARD:
There was no money on him or in his wallet, only some American traveler's checks. Was that custom-ary with him, Captain Morgan?

MORGAN:
He had sixty bucks in it.

RENARD:
What became of it?

MORGAN:
I took it.

RENARD:
Why?

[MORGAN:
Because he owed me eight hundred and forty dollars.

RENARD:
> So at least you didn't kill him, did you?][50]

MORGAN:
> So it would seem.

RENARD:
> But unfortunately for you, someone did. As a result of which, you took it on yourself to collect a part of the debt. You have this money now?

MORGAN:
> Yes.

RENARD (extending his hand):
> If you please.

Morgan takes his whole roll from his pocket, not only the money he took out of Johnson's wallet, but his own roll too. He begins to count the sixty dollars onto the desk. Renard continues to hold his hand out.

RENARD (with more emphasis):
> If you please, Captain.

MORGAN:
> Some of this is mine.

RENARD:
> How do we know that?

Morgan stares at him a moment, shrugs, tosses the money across the desk. Renard takes it and puts it into the drawer.

RENARD:
> Thank you. Do not be concerned. This money is impounded by a government which, like your own, is at peace with the world. If your claim is just, it will be discharged.

He turns to Marie.

[RENARD:
Miss—?][51]

COYO (opening Marie's passport and comparing Marie with it):
Browning, Marie. American, age twenty-two. How long have you been in Fort de France?

[MARIE:
Since this—this afternoon.][52]

COYO:
Residence?

MARIE:
The Hotel Marquis.

COYO:
You come from where?

MARIE:
Trinidad. Port of Spain.

RENARD:
And before that, from where, mademoiselle? From home, perhaps?

MARIE:
No. From Rio.

RENARD:
Alone?

MARIE (hesitates):
Yes.

RENARD:
Why did you get off here?

MARIE:
To buy a new hat.

Coyo steps forward and slaps Marie. Morgan is watching all this. He sees Marie take the slap without turning a hair. She is smoking a cigarette. She turns and puts the cigarette into an ashtray on the desk, takes her hat off, and holds it out for Renard to see the label.

[MARIE:
Maybe you'll believe me now.][53]

RENARD:
I have never doubted you, mademoiselle. It is only your tone that was objectionable. I'll ask you again. Why did you get off here?

MARIE:
I didn't have money enough to go any further.

RENARD:
That's better. Where were you when the shooting occurred?

[MORGAN (to Marie):
You don't have to answer this stuff.

COYO (to Morgan):
Shut up, you.

MORGAN (to Marie):
Don't answer him.

Coyo takes a step toward Morgan, threateningly.

MORGAN (to Coyo):
That's right. Slap me.][54]

RENARD:
Come, come, Captain. This is not a brawl. We merely wish to get to the bottom of this affair.

[MORGAN:
You won't do it by slapping Americans. That's bad luck.

RENARD:

>An American who interferes with the police of a foreign government is already in bad luck. That will do now.][55] If we need to question you further, you will be available at the hotel?

MORGAN:

>I'm not likely to go anywhere as long as you have my money and my passport both.

RENARD:

>Your passport will be returned to you. As for the money, if it is yours, that will arrange itself in good time.

MORGAN:

>Maybe I'd better see the American consul and get him to help you arrange it.

RENARD:

>That is your privilege. By the way, what are your sympathies?

MORGAN:

>Minding my own business.

RENARD:

>May I suggest—?

[MORGAN:

>And I don't need any advice about continuing to do it either. (To Marie.) Come on. Let's get out of here.][56]

Morgan and Marie exit.

DISSOLVE TO:

22.　EXT. NARROW STREET　　　　A FEW MINUTES LATER

[Sound of music from little bistro in basement. Morgan and Marie come around corner. Marie stops and looks into cafe.

MARIE:

>I could use a drink.

MORGAN:
So could I.][57]

They exit.

23.   INT. BISTRO
Place crowded with Martiniquais and sailors. Couples dancing in small space surrounded by tables. Morgan and Marie enter and make their way to bar in rear.

[BARTENDER (in French):
What are you going to have?

Morgan, putting hand in pocket, grins and shakes his head.

MORGAN:
Just looking around.

MARIE:
No money?

MORGAN:
Those cops cleaned me out.

MARIE:
Guess we'll have to wait till we get back to the hotel.

MORGAN:
They're closed up tight.

MARIE:
I forgot.

She turns to survey room, putting arms on bar.

MORGAN:
Picking out somebody?

MARIE:
This has been a pretty large day for me. I really need a drink. (As Morgan looks at her.) You don't mind, do you?

MORGAN (taking out cigarette):
  No. Go ahead.][58]

Marie, putting hand on his shoulder, pushes him back a
little so she can look at other end of room, then walks out,
taking cigarette from Morgan as she passes. Morgan, taking out another cigarette, watches her as she strolls
among the tables. Several men give her the eye, but she
pays no attention to them, until she passes a handsome
young French naval ensign, giving a light to a friend.
Marie, stooping, lights cigarette from extended match and
continues on her way to dance floor. Young ensign, looking after her, rises with a grin at his companion and joins
Marie. He asks her to dance. Marie looks him over, then
accepts, and as they dance away she looks at Morgan over
her partner's shoulder. Morgan, lighting cigarette, walks
toward door. As he exits, we

                                    DISSOLVE TO:

24.   INT. MORGAN'S SITTING ROOM   HALF AN HOUR LATER
Morgan, opening door, looks at Marie, who stands in hall
with a bottle under her arm.

MARIE:
  Hello.

[MORGAN:
  Hello.][59]

He walks back and sits down at table. Marie, closing door,
leans back against it and looks at him.

MARIE:
  You're sore, aren't you?

MORGAN:
  Why should I be?

MARIE (coming over):
  I didn't behave very well, did I?

MORGAN:
You did all right. You got a bottle, didn't you?

MARIE (starting to open bottle):
You're sore, aren't you?

MORGAN:
Look. Get this straight. I don't give a—

MARIE:
I know. You don't give a whoop what I do. But when I do it, you get sore. (Smiles.) You told me to, you know.

MORGAN:
I told you?

MARIE:
You said go ahead, didn't you?

[MORGAN:
You were pretty good at it, too.][60]

MARIE:
Thanks. (Goes to wall cupboard, returns with two glasses.) Would you rather I wouldn't?

MORGAN:
Wouldn't what?

MARIE (pouring drinks):
Do things like that.

MORGAN:
Why ask me?

MARIE:
I'd like to know.

[MORGAN (picking up drink):
Of all the screwy dames—

MARIE:
All right. I won't do it anymore.][61]

MORGAN:
Look, I didn't ask you—

[MARIE:
Don't worry. I'm not giving up anything I care about. It's like shooting fish in a barrel anyway.

MORGAN:
What?

MARIE:
These men— (Laughs.) They're all a bunch of— (Laughs again.) I'm a fine one to talk. The pot calling the kettle black.

She picks up glass and walks out door.][62]

25. INT. HALLWAY
Marie crosses hall, unlocks door of her room, and exits.
                                                    DISSOLVE TO:

26. INT. MARIE'S BEDROOM   A LITTLE LATER
Marie sitting at dressing table, brushing her hair. She has changed to negligee. She hears somebody opening door in sitting room.

MARIE:
Who is it?

[MORGAN'S VOICE:
Me.

MARIE:
What's on your mind?

27. INT. MARIE'S SITTING ROOM
Morgan, closing door, takes bottle out from under arm.

MORGAN:
I brought your bottle over.

MARIE'S VOICE:
Thanks.

Morgan, setting bottle on table, looks around room. There are several framed snapshots on walls. Morgan goes and looks at a couple of them. In one, Marie, wearing a bathing suit, stands beside a shapely brunette who wears bathing suit marked Miss Miami. In the other, Marie stands beside another shapely blonde who wears bathing suit marked Miss Palm Beach. On the other walls hang snaps taken by professional photographers on the beach at Rio, Buenos Aires, Trinidad, etc. Marie and an Argentine girl sitting in a wheelchair. Marie sitting under an umbrella, with a handsome young escort.

28.   INT. MARIE'S BEDROOM
Marie, leaning back in chair and looking through doorway, sees what Morgan is doing.

MARIE:
There's a scrapbook on the table.

Morgan picks it up, looking through album as he comes through doorway.

MORGAN (looking at clippings):
You've been in quite a few of these contests.

MARIE (nodding):
Always a runner-up.

Morgan walks over and looks down at her, studying her with a thoughtful eye.

MORGAN:
What are you going to do, Slim?

MARIE:
I was just going to ask you the same question, Steve.

MORGAN:
How long have you been away from home?

MARIE (brushing her hair):
This is about the time for it, isn't it?

MORGAN:
> What?

MARIE:
> The story of my life. Where shall I begin?

MORGAN (sitting down on bed):
> I've got a pretty fair idea already.

MARIE:
> Who told you?

MORGAN:
> You did.

MARIE:
> Go on.

MORGAN:
> That slap in the face you took.

MARIE:
> What about it?

MORGAN:
> You hardly blinked an eye. That takes a lot of practice. Yeah, I know a lot about you, Slim.

MARIE:
> Hm-m. Next time I get slapped I better do something about it.

Morgan, rising, picks up bottle of perfume from dressing table, smells stopper.

MARIE:
> Remind you of somebody, Steve?

MORGAN (putting bottle down):
> A little.

Marie, picking up bottle, puts some of the perfume behind her ears, touching stopper to her throat.

MORGAN (drawing a deep breath):
>It's nice.

He sits down on bed and looks at her with a frank, appreciative eye.

MARIE (after a moment):
>I'm tired, Steve. Think I'll turn in.

MORGAN (rising):
>Not a bad idea.

He exits into sitting room.

MARIE:
>Take the bottle along if you want.

MORGAN'S VOICE (in sitting room):
>I'll just take a nightcap.][63]

DISSOLVE TO:

29.   INT. MORGAN'S SITTING ROOM   TEN MINUTES LATER
Morgan, sitting at table, is finishing drink. There is a knock at door and Marie enters in doorway.

[MARIE:
>Steve.

MORGAN:
>I thought you were going to bed.

MARIE:
>Are you going to see the American consul in the morning?

MORGAN:
>Sure.

MARIE (coming in):
>Think it'll do any good?

MORGAN:
>Not for now.

Marie, sitting down on couch, starts to take off her slipper.

MARIE:
Who was the girl, Steve?

MORGAN:
What girl?

MARIE:
The one who left you with such pleasant memories. You don't think much of women, do you, Steve? (Morgan doesn't answer, and Marie starts to remove stockings.) She must have been quite a gal. I guess we're both in the same boat—only I don't feel so bad about it.

She takes some bills out of foot of stocking and goes over to Morgan.

MARIE:
You can use this, can't you? (Holding out bills.) Here.

Morgan looks at money and shakes his head.

MORGAN:
Thanks just the same.

MARIE:
I thought they cleaned you out?

MORGAN:
I thought you said you were broke?

MARIE:
Oh, I always try to keep enough to be independent of certain situations. Sure you can't use this?

MORGAN:
You need it more than I do.

Marie, looking at him, turns and walks over to door, where she pushes up transom.

MARIE (lowering her voice as she returns):
Going to take that de Gaullist job?

MORGAN:
I don't know. Depends.

MARIE:
We flew over Devil's Island. Doesn't look like such a high-class resort.

MORGAN:
That's what I hear.

MARIE:
I wouldn't take a chance on it for fifty dollars.

MORGAN:
You'll be taking a chance on it for nothing if you don't keep your nose out of it.

He walks over to door and pulls down transom again. Marie, watching him, smiles.

MARIE (studying him):
You don't like to take favors, do you?

MORGAN:
Not any better than I like doing them. (Lighting cigarette.) Anything else you'd like to know? I'm not much for keeping photos—or scrapbooks.

MARIE:
You're not very hard to figure, Steve—only at times. Sometimes I know exactly what you're going to say—most of the time. The other times— (sitting down in his lap) the other times, you're just a stinker.

MORGAN:
What's all this for?

MARIE:
Well, somebody has to make the first move.

She kisses him.

MORGAN:
> Why did you do that?

MARIE:
> I've been wondering whether I'd like it.

MORGAN:
> What's the decision?

MARIE:
> I don't know yet.

She kisses him again, and this time Morgan puts his arms around her and returns the kiss.

MARIE (rising):
> I thought you wouldn't take anything from anybody?

MORGAN:
> That's different.

MARIE (holding up money):
> Changed your mind about this, too?

MORGAN:
> No.

MARIE:
> I can't figure it.

MORGAN:
> What?

MARIE (looking at money):
> This belongs to me—so do my lips. I don't see any difference.

MORGAN:
> Who was the fellow?

MARIE:
> What fellow?

MORGAN:
> The one that left you with such a pleasant viewpoint. You don't think much of men, do you? He must have been quite a guy.

MARIE:
> We live and learn—but slow.

She puts money away, walks over, and picks up footgear, starting toward door.

MORGAN (grinning):
> You're sore, aren't you?

MARIE (leaning against door):
> I've been sore ever since I met you. One look and you had me placed. You didn't see me take Johnson's wallet, but you knew I had it. I brought that bottle up here to make you feel cheap. But I haven't made a dent in you. I'm the one who feels cheap. I've never felt so cheap in my life.

MORGAN:
> What did I do?

MARIE (ironical, bitter):
> Nothing. That's the whole trouble. What's more, you don't have to do anything. Not a thing. Oh, maybe just whistle. (Opening hall door.) You know how to whistle, don't you, Steve? You just put your lips together and blow.

She smiles and walks out, closing door behind her. As Morgan looks after her, we][64]

FADE OUT

FADE IN

30.   EXT. NEGRO CABIN IN OUTSKIRTS
FORT DE FRANCE   NEXT MORNING

Little colored boy sitting on oxcart in front of cabin. He sees automobile coming around bend in road. He looks toward cabin and pretends to call chickens.

COLORED BOY:
   Chick—chick—chick—

It is a signal to his mother, who opens door of cabin and looks out [as automobile stops in front. It is a French command car, and it contains four armed sailors.

SAILOR (in French):
   Did you see two white men pass on this road?

COLORED WOMAN (in French):
   Not today.

SAILOR (in French, to boy):
   And you?

Boy shakes his head. Sailors exit in car. Mother smiles at boy and closes door of cabin.]⁶⁵

31.   INT. CABIN
Negro woman closing door. We see Beauclerc lying on cot, his rudely bandaged right leg resting on pillow. Mrs. Beauclerc sits on edge of bed, fanning away flies above her husband's face. Gerard standing nearby. Morgan turning from window in relief. Gerard wipes forehead and throat with handkerchief.

[BEAUCLERC (to Morgan):
   Yesterday you very definitely refused to have anything to do with us. Why have you changed your mind?

MORGAN:
   Yesterday I had eight hundred and twenty-five dollars in sight. Today—thanks to you and your Vichy friends—fifty dollars is fifty dollars.

MRS. BEAUCLERC:
   I wouldn't trust him.

MORGAN (without resentment):
   I usually do what I'm paid to do.

Gerard silently nods head to Beauclerc behind Morgan's back.

BEAUCLERC:
I'm sure of that, Captain Morgan.

MORGAN:
Where is this place you want me to take you to?

GERARD:
It is the little islet of Anguilla—about forty kilometers on the way to Guadeloupe.

MORGAN:
I know where it is. (To Beauclerc.) Who you running out there?

BEAUCLERC:
Nobody. We want you to pick up two people there and bring them here.

MORGAN:
I can't land anybody after dark. The port closes at sunset now. They'd nail us all.

GERARD:
We've arranged that. A bateau will meet you outside the breakwater and take them off. Then you can wait till daylight to come on.

MORGAN:
Okay. You be in that bateau. (To Beauclerc.) Where'll these people be?

BEAUCLERC:
I'll show you when we get there.

MORGAN:
You're not going with that leg.

MRS. BEAUCLERC:
Of course not. He can't put his weight on it.

MORGAN:
> You'd only be in the way.

BEAUCLERC (making gesture of resignation):
> You come along the lee shore of Anguilla from the south. They'll be watching for you, and when you put on your running lights, they'll answer it. You'll see two flashlights—one held above the other.

MORGAN:
> There's a little jetty in there, isn't there?

GERARD:
> That's where they'll be. The password is "Norlarie."

MORGAN:
> "Norlarie." (To Beauclerc.) Can you pay me now?

MRS. BEAUCLERC:
> You see how much he trusts us?

Beauclerc takes out packet of paper francs and counts them into Morgan's hand.

GERARD:
> Harry, if you knew what this means to us—

BEAUCLERC:
> Not only to us—but to France.

MORGAN (going over to light to recount money):
> I don't want to know.

GERARD:
> We won't forget it.

BEAUCLERC:
> I knew you were on our side.

MORGAN:
> Sure I am. I'm on any side that pays me. (Indicating Beauclerc's wounded leg.) Had a doctor look at that?

BEAUCLERC (shaking head):
> They know I'm wounded. They're watching all the doctors who are friendly to us.

MORGAN:
> Who told you to put this pillow under it?

MRS. BEAUCLERC:
> I did! What's wrong with it?

BEAUCLERC:
> It doesn't hurt so much that way.

MORGAN (removing pillow):
> You'll have to grin and take it. Unless you want gangrene to set in.

MRS. BEAUCLERC:
> Are you a doctor?

MORGAN:
> No. But I've handled quite a few gunshot wounds.

He starts out with Frenchy.

BEAUCLERC:
> Bon voyage!

MRS. BEAUCLERC (as they exit):
> Bon voyage to our money!][66]

DISSOLVE TO:

32.   INT. CAFE   AN HOUR LATER
[Morgan eating lunch. Gerard enters with pot of coffee. As he pours it into cup, Morgan sees Marie descending stairway. He waves to her.

MARIE (coming over):
> Hello, Frenchy.

GERARD (bowing):
> Mademoiselle!

He exits and Marie stops by Morgan's chair.

MARIE (shoving finger inside his collar):
How are you, Steve?

MORGAN (pulling out chair):
How'd you sleep?

MARIE (stretching luxuriously):
Wonderful!

Waitress enters as Marie sits down.

MARIE (to Morgan):
Can I start with a rum swizzle?

MORGAN:
Too early.

MARIE:
Just enough to fill an elephant's ear.

MORGAN (to waitress):
Bring her some breakfast, Rosalie.

ROSALIE (as she goes):
Yes, m'sieur.

MORGAN:
Could you get packed in time for the afternoon plane?

MARIE:
Why?

Morgan takes out envelope and gives it to her.

MORGAN:
There's a ticket to San Juan.

MARIE:
San Juan? What'll I do in Puerto Rico?

MORGAN:
Better town than this any day.

MARIE (after a moment):
Where did you make the raise?

MORGAN:
No fooling, Slim. This is a good place to be from.

MARIE:
So you took that job?

MORGAN:
I got the dough from Frenchy.

MARIE:
Funny, San Juan is just fifty-eight dollars as the crow flies.

Morgan finishes his coffee.

MORGAN (rising):
Drop me a card if you get stuck there.

MARIE:
Sure. X marks my room. Send fifty more.

MORGAN:
May stop by and pick you up on my way home. (Stoops and kisses her.) Keep your nose clean.

MARIE:
You do the same. (Draws his head down and kisses him.) Thanks, Steve.

MORGAN:
So long.

He rumples her hair and starts out toward front. Marie looks after him, her eyes slowly filling with tears.][67]

DISSOLVE TO:

FADE IN

33.   EXT. FORT DE FRANCE   DOCK   LATE THAT AFTERNOON
Morgan's ship, the *Queen Conch*, tied up. Morgan is working on engine. A plane passes overhead, the Pan Ameri-

can for Miami. Morgan looks up, watches it pass, believing that Marie is on it. Eddy enters on dock, longer, blearier, drunker than ever. He jumps down on deck and almost breaks in half.

EDDY:
   Hello, Harry. How's everything?

MORGAN:
   Fine. Didn't I tell you to stay at the hotel until I got back?

Eddy sits down in fishing chair and stretches out his legs.

EDDY:
   I knew you were going out.

MORGAN:
   Who told you?

[EDDY:
   You can't fool me, Harry. I can tell it just as plain.

MORGAN (coming out of engine hatch):
   Well, *you're* not going.][68]

EDDY:
   Can I have a little one, Harry? Just enough to fill a hen's ear?

MORGAN:
   Come on—get off.

[EDDY:
   You can't go without a mate.

MORGAN (coming aft):
   Do you think having a rummy on board makes any difference? (Jerking Eddy out of chair.) Get off of her. You're poison to me—][69]

EDDY:
   What's the matter, Harry? There's no sense getting plugged with me.

MORGAN:
Get off of her—

EDDY:
Aw, take it easy—

Morgan hits him on the face. Eddy sags down against dock, then, holding his face, he rises and climbs up onto dock.

EDDY:
I wouldn't do a thing like that to you, Harry.

MORGAN:
You're darn right you wouldn't. I'm not going to carry you. That's all.

EDDY:
Well, what did you have to hit me for?

MORGAN:
So you'd believe it.

EDDY:
You aren't treating me square.

MORGAN:
Who did you ever treat square, [you rummy?][70] You'd double-cross your own mother. You told me so yourself.

EDDY:
I was only kidding.

He starts to walk off down the dock looking longer than a day without breakfast. Then he turns and comes back.

[EDDY:
Say, Harry—will you let me take a couple of dollars?

MORGAN (handing him a bill):
Here.

EDDY (brightening):
> Okay. I always knew you were my pal. Harry, why don't you carry me?

MORGAN:
> You're bad luck.][71]

EDDY:
> You're just plugged. Never mind, old pal. You'll be glad to see me yet.

Morgan looks after Eddy as the latter walks off down the dock, then goes back into engine hatch.

DISSOLVE TO:

34. EXT. QUEEN CONCH AT SEA   LATER THAT NIGHT
She is drifting in a heavy fog off islet where Morgan has a rendezvous. Morgan has just shut off motors and is throwing hook overboard.

35. INT. WHEELHOUSE
Morgan enters, opens locker, and takes out a twelve-gauge pump gun and a Winchester thirty-thirty and hangs them up in their cases right over the wheel where he can reach them. Taking pump gun out of case, he works her a few times, then fills her up with shells and pumps one in the barrel. Then he puts a shell in the barrel of the Winchester and fills up the magazine. He shoves Winchester back in the case. He hears something in the direction of the cabin. He takes thirty-eight Special out of waistband of trousers and walks forward.

36. EXT. DECK QUEEN CONCH
Morgan enters and stops as he sees cabin hatch is opening. He cocks six-shooter.

MORGAN:
> All right. Come on out.

Eddy cautiously sticks his head out of hatch.

[EDDY:
Don't shoot, Harry. It's only me.

MORGAN (putting gun away):
How did you get back on her?

EDDY:
Well, I walked up the street, bought a couple of bottles, and sneaked back in here when you were working on the engine.

Morgan grins in spite of himself.

MORGAN:
Come on out of there—and bring the bottles along.

EDDY (grinning):
I knew you would carry me, Harry.

MORGAN:
Carry you nothing. You're not even on the crew list. I have a good mind to make you jump overboard now.

EDDY (laughing):
You're an old joker, Harry. Us Key Westers ought to stick together when we are in trouble.

MORGAN:
How d'you know I'm in trouble?

EDDY:
You can't fool me. I always know.

MORGAN:
You with your mouth. Who's going to trust your mouth when you're drunk?

He walks into wheelhouse and Eddy follows him.

37.   INT. WHEELHOUSE
Morgan enters with Eddy.

EDDY:
   I'm a good man, Harry. You just put me to the test
   and see what a good man I am.

MORGAN (sitting down on locker):
   Give me those bottles.

Eddy reluctantly hands them over. One is open. Morgan
takes a drink from it and puts it forward by the wheel.
Eddy stands there and Morgan looks at him.

EDDY (looking around):
   What's the matter, Harry? What are you looking at
   me like that for?

MORGAN:
   Nothing. Just a joke that neither of us knows the answer to.

EDDY:
   What joke?

MORGAN:
   Whether you'll hold together or not.

EDDY (quickly):
   I'm a good man. You know I am. (Suddenly sober.)
   Say—what's goin' on? What're we gonna do?

MORGAN:
   I don't know, yet. Haven't got it all figured out, yet.

Takes another drink out of bottle. Stands looking at the
fog on shore.

EDDY (after a moment):
   Harry—

Morgan doesn't answer.

EDDY:
   Why don't you ask me if I've got a mouth on me?

MORGAN (without turning his head):
>   You've had enough for now. I'll give you one later on.

EDDY (wetting his lips):
>   Can't I have just a little one now?

MORGAN:
>   No. I don't want you to be rum-dumb—I want you to be rum-brave.

Then Eddy sees rifle and shotgun hanging over wheel.

EDDY:
>   What the dickens is the matter?

MORGAN:
>   Nothing.

EDDY:
>   What's all the darn guns for?

MORGAN:
>   In case we see a shark or something.

EDDY:
>   A shark! At night? Look—what's goin' on here?

MORGAN (taking another drink):
>   I always carry them on board to shoot birds that bother the baits, or sharks, when we are cruising along the keys.

EDDY:
>   What's the matter, darn it, what's the matter?

MORGAN:
>   Nothing. (Takes another drink.) We are going to do a little job. I'll tell you what to do when it's time.

EDDY (excited and happy):
>   You couldn't have anybody better than me, Harry. I'm the man for anything.

Morgan looks at him—tall, lanky, and bleary—and he doesn't say anything.

EDDY (after a moment):
 Listen, Harry—would you give me just one? I don't want to get the shakes.

Morgan hands him the bottle.

MORGAN:
 I don't want you rum-brave until I tell you. Make it a short one.

He looks toward shore.][72]

38. INT. WHEELHOUSE QUEEN CONCH   OUTSIDE COVE
Morgan flashes on his running lights, then turns them off. There is an answering signal from shore—two lights—one held above the other. Morgan turns to Eddy, who sits on locker.

[EDDY (excitedly):
 Okay, Harry?

MORGAN:
 Get the hook aboard, you big brave man.][73]

Eddy goes forward and Morgan starts his motors. Then he goes forward.

39. [EXT. DECK OF QUEEN CONCH
Eddy is vainly trying to get anchor aboard. He's too weak to do much good. Morgan enters and gives him a hand.

MORGAN:
 Listen, we are going in to pick up two guys. You take the wheel when I tell you to and do what I tell you to. Come on. Get that hook up.

EDDY (as they get anchor on board):
 Harry, can I have one of those now?

MORGAN (starting back toward wheelhouse):
I'll give you one in a minute.

EDDY:
I'm a good man. You'll see.

MORGAN:
You're a rummy.][74]

40.   INT. WHEELHOUSE
[Morgan enters with Eddy at his heels. He takes a drink from bottle and hands it to Eddy. As Eddy drinks, Morgan shoves in clutch and starts in toward shore.

MORGAN (jerks bottle from Eddy's mouth):
Listen to me. When I give you the word, cut her and put the wheel over and let her drift stern first in toward the jetty. As soon as she comes around, put her in gear and keep your hand on the clutch. Two people are to come aboard. When I give you the word, hook her up quick, and get out of there. If more than two people try to board us, or anything happens to me, hook her up and head out to sea. You can hold the wheelhouse against them with the shotgun until you can make a deal, or at least find out what the score is.

EDDY:
Alone? If anything happens to you? Then what do I do?

MORGAN:
How do I know? You invited yourself on this trip. I didn't.

EDDY (trembling, but trying to pull himself together):
All right, but you better give me another drink.

MORGAN (handing him the bottle):
Here.

Eddy takes the bottle and drinks. Morgan snatches it away, strikes the cork in with his palm, and puts the bottle away.][75]

41.　　EXT. THE JETTY

The boat drifts up to the jetty, where three dim figures are waiting. They are Paul, Helene, and a guide.

GUIDE (in French):
　　Who's there?

[MORGAN:
　　"Norlarie."

GUIDE (in French):
　　Throw me your line.

MORGAN (catching hold of the jetty):
　　Never mind that. Put your people aboard.

GUIDE (to others, in French):
　　They have sent an American.

MORGAN (impatiently):
　　Come on. Come on.

Two of the dark figures reluctantly approach the boat. Helene starts to get down into it. She will have to jump, and hesitates. Morgan does not yet see that she is a woman. He holds out his hand. She takes it and jumps down into the boat. Only when he touches her hand does he realize she is a woman.

MORGAN (in surprise):
　　Say, what's this?

HELENE (in English):
　　Thank you.

MORGAN (to the guide):
　　They didn't say anything about a woman.

GUIDE (in French):
I don't speak English. Here is Monsieur de Bursac.

MORGAN:
All right, jump in.

Paul jumps down into the boat.

MORGAN (over his shoulder to Eddy):
Hook her up. Let's get out of here.][76]

The boat starts to gather speed.

42. GROUP SHOT
Morgan, Helene, and Paul at the stern. The boat is going fast.

[PAUL (in English):
Permit me, Captain. My wife, Madame de Bursac. She is an American, too.

MORGAN:
I don't care what she is. What did you want to bring your wife here for? What kind of a war are you guys fighting, lugging your wives around with you?

HELENE (bristling):
What business is it of yours?

MORGAN:
An American, huh? Well, nothing like a little cheese-cake for a touch of color. How come you didn't bring along a photographer?

PAUL (angrily):
Who are you?

HELENE:
Where is Beauclerc?

MORGAN:
He got in a little trouble. Come into the wheelhouse. It's blowing up outside.

HELENE:
There'll be some more blowing up when we get to Fort de France, too. Of all the insolence!

PAUL (stiffly, to Morgan):
We will stay here. We will be quite comfortable, thank you.

MORGAN (as he goes forward):
Suit yourself.][77]

DISSOLVE TO:

43.   INT. WHEELHOUSE
Morgan is steering. Eddy dozing on seat. Morgan sees something ahead, reacts in alarm, cuts the switch. The SOUND of the engine STOPS. The boat drifts on.

[EDDY (sitting up):
What's wrong?

Morgan crouches over the wheel, tense, staring ahead into the darkness, Eddy beside him. As they listen, the SOUND of another boat, moving slow, comes from ahead.

EDDY:
Did you get a sight of it?

MORGAN:
I didn't have to. Don't you know that engine? It's the patrol boat.

As they listen tensely, the SOUND of the other engine STOPS. Morgan quickly takes the rifle from the rack on the bulkhead.][78]

EDDY:
Here! You can't fight those guys.

MORGAN (jacking a shell into the rifle):
What's the matter? This is where you ought to be telling me how good you are.

[EDDY (pulling himself together):
    All right. What do you want me to do?

MORGAN:
    Just what you did before. Put her in gear and be
    ready to pour the coal to her when I give you the
    word.

EDDY (trembling):
    Maybe I'd better have that other drink now.

MORGAN (about to exit):
    What other drink?

Morgan exits. Eddy stares ahead into the darkness, fum-
bling around for the bottle, trembling, frightened, but
trying to hold himself together. He cannot find the
bottle.][79]

44.   GROUP SHOT   AT STERN
       Paul and Helene have risen as Morgan enters with the
       rifle.

[PAUL:
    What is it?

MORGAN:
    It's the patrol ship.

PAUL:
    What shall we do?

MORGAN (staring into the darkness toward the invisible
ship):
    Nothing. Get down below the gunwale and stay
    there.

PAUL (indicates the rifle):
    And you will try to resist with that? You'll get us all
    killed.

MORGAN:
> Look—will you get down there and shut up? Both of you. You just save France. Let me save my ship.][80]

Paul and Helene crouch below the gunwale. Morgan crouches, staring into the darkness, the rifle ready. The patrol boat's searchlight comes on, moves across the water toward them, stops, swings back in the other direction, stops, then moves again across the water toward them, drawing nearer and nearer until it picks up the boat. As it does so, Paul springs up and stands on the coaming with his arms raised above his head.

[PAUL (in French):
> We surrender. Don't—

Morgan knocks Paul down into the boat. Helene starts toward Morgan with tigress fury.

HELENE:
> You big bully!

MORGAN (shoving her away):
> If you want to surrender, jump overboard. (To Eddy.) Hook her up.

The boat surges forward. Morgan fires at the searchlight, misses, jacks another shell into the rifle. Paul tries to rise. As he does so, a burst of fire comes from the patrol boat. Paul is hit and cries out. Morgan shoots out the searchlight. As he turns to run to the wheel, he sees Paul sprawled on the seat with Helene bending over him.

HELENE (in alarm):
> Paul! Are you hurt?

Morgan stoops to examine Paul's wound. He has been shot in the right shoulder.

MORGAN:
> So that's how you're saving France—by surrendering to the first Vichy cop that yells "Stop" at you.

PAUL (weakly):
Please do as I say. It is for the best.

MORGAN (to Helene):
You see what happens when you lug women around?
(Pointing to Paul.) Get him off the seat. He's bleeding
all over my cushion.

HELENE:
What kind of a man are you—talking about your silly
cushion? Why don't you do something for him?

MORGAN (as he goes forward):
I haven't got time right now.][81]

DISSOLVE TO

45.   OFF SHORE   DAWN
The *Queen Conch* has stopped. Gerard and another man
pull up beside it in a bateau. Aboard the *Queen Conch*,
Paul lies on the floor of cockpit, a crude bandage around
his shoulder. Helene is beside him, looking wan and
dazed. [Morgan enters and catches painter.

MORGAN:
Hello, Frenchy.

GERARD (anxiously):
What happened?

MORGAN:
Your friend got shot up a little.

HELENE (rouses):
Who are these people?

MORGAN (to Helene):
This is Frenchy Gerard, the guy that hired me to
bring you here. (To Gerard.) All right, Frenchy. Take
them off.

HELENE:
I don't understand.

MORGAN:
This is all of it. The end of the line.

HELENE (looks about at the desolate shore):
Here? Like this? Aren't you going to take us any far-
ther?

MORGAN:
This is as far as I go.

HELENE:
But you can't. You can't—

MORGAN (to Gerard):
Look. Get them out of my boat. And you better talk
to them. If this is the sort of people you are hoping
to save Martinique with, no wonder the Vichy cops
run you ragged. (Over his shoulder to Eddy.) Come
here.

Eddy enters, a little wobbly in the legs.

EDDY:
Hello, Frenchy.

MORGAN:
Give us a hand here.

Morgan, Eddy, and Gerard lift Paul into the bateau. Helene is dazed. She stumbles as she tries to follow Paul.
Morgan catches her by the hand before she falls and helps
her into the skiff. Gerard and the other oarsman row
away.

MORGAN (to Eddy):
All right. Hook her up.

Eddy goes to the wheelhouse. The boat starts. Morgan
turns away. He pauses, sniffs, as if he had suddenly
smelled something, turns his head from side to side, sniff-

ing, raises the hand with which he had helped Helene into the boat, sniffs at it, smells the faint scent which she had left, dips hand in water to wash it off.][82]

FADE OUT

FADE IN

46. INT. CAFE   LATER THAT MORNING
Place is practically deserted. Morgan, coming in with Eddy, pauses blankly as he sees Marie standing by piano, listening to Cricket rehearse a number with orchestra.

[MARIE (seeing him):
   Hello, Steve.

EDDY (turning to Morgan):
   I thought you said she pulled out?

MORGAN:
   Why didn't you take that plane?

MARIE:
   I decided to wait for you.

She puts hand in his pocket and takes out package of cigarettes.

MORGAN (angrily):
   I went to a lot of trouble to get you out of here.][83]

MARIE:
   That's why I didn't go.

[As Morgan looks at her, she takes some bills out of pocket.

MARIE:
   I got a refund on the ticket. Want me to keep it for you?

EDDY (seeing money):
   Listen, Harry. Could I—?

MORGAN:

You've had enough to last you a week. (To Marie.) Don't buy him nothing but beer.

As he turns to go, Frenchy enters.

MORGAN:

Have any trouble getting them ashore?

GERARD:

No. But Madame refused to let us take them to that place in the country. She said it was too far. He would die before he got there.

MORGAN:

What does she know?

GERARD:

He is very badly wounded, Harry. Anybody can see that.][84]

MORGAN:

I looked at it. The bullet hit the gunwale first and was practically spent. All you have to do is to get some-body to take it out. [(To Marie.) Had your breakfast?

MARIE (nodding):

But I'll have a cup of coffee with you.

Morgan starts toward table in rear, but Frenchy follows him.][85]

GERARD:

Couldn't you do it for us?

[MORGAN:

Me? Listen, I'm hotter right now than any doctor. Don't you think they recognized my ship? Why, the minute I walk out of here they'll be right on my trail—

GERARD:
I thought about that. That's why I brought them here.

MORGAN (stopping in horror):
You what?

MARIE:
You brought them here?

MORGAN (pointing to big goldfish bowl):
Why didn't you stick them in that and be done with it?

GERARD:
I know it sounds crazy, but what could I do? If that man dies, our only hope of saving Martinique is gone.

MORGAN:
Listen, I don't owe you anything, Frenchy. I did what you paid me for, didn't I? I pay for everything I get around here, don't I? Ask her. (He gestures at old cashier behind grill;][86] turning on Marie.) You see what you got into by sticking around?

MARIE:
I'm willing to pull out any time you are.

[MORGAN (turning to cashier):
Make out our bills. (To Eddy.) Go upstairs and get our things packed.

EDDY:
Where we going?

MORGAN:
Never mind. Hurry up.

CASHIER (looking at ledger):
Your bill, Captain Morgan, being somewhat in arrears, amounts to six thousand three hundred and fifty-six francs.

MORGAN (to Marie):
 We haven't got half that, have we?

Marie shakes her head, whereupon the cashier smiles.

CASHIER:
 I think M'sieur Gerard will be glad to dismiss the whole matter if you will—

GERARD (eagerly):
 By all means.][87]

Morgan motions at Marie.

MORGAN:
 Throw her bill in with it?

GERARD:
 Sure thing.

MORGAN:
 All I have to do is to get the bullet out and put a dressing on it?

GERARD:
 That's all.

[MORGAN (to cashier):
 Put some water on to boil. I'll give you a probe to sterilize.

OLD CASHIER (as she exits):
 Voilà, mon capitaine.

MORGAN (starting toward stairway):
 I'll go up and get my kit.

MARIE:
 What can I do?

MORGAN:
 Go up and pack your things. (As she exits up stairs, he turns to Gerard.) Where are they?

GERARD (pointing to the floor):
Down in the wine cellar.

MORGAN:
You poor sap. That's the first place they'll look.

GERARD:
I know. We all crazy except you, Harry—and I think you are a little crazy, too.

MORGAN (as he goes upstairs):
You said it.][88]

DISSOLVE TO:

47.   INT. WINE CELLAR OF CAFE   A LITTLE LATER
Gerard and Morgan descending stairway. We can HEAR Cricket at piano OVERHEAD. Morgan carries a ship's medical kit. Gerard, lighting a candle, leads him through aisle in wine racks to far end of cellar. Here he pushes aside an old sideboard, disclosing door. He opens door, motioning Morgan to precede him.

48.   INT. BEDROOM NO. 1   OLD SERVANT'S QUARTERS
The room is empty. Morgan looks around curiously as he enters with Gerard.

[MORGAN:
What's this?

GERARD:
Some old servant's quarters.][89]

He leads Morgan through bathroom into another bedroom.

49.   INT. BEDROOM NO. 2
Paul lying unconscious on cot. Helene sitting on chair nearby, fanning him. She rises as Gerard enters with Morgan.

HELENE (recognizing Morgan):
What do you want?

[MORGAN:
    Hello, Cheesecake.

HELENE:
    Where's the doctor?

GERARD:
    Please be patient, madame. We will get one as soon
    as—

HELENE:
    Patient! You think I can sit here and watch my hus-
    band die—just because of a pack of cowardly—

MORGAN:
    Quit that yelling. (Starting to remove crude bandage
    from Paul's shoulder) He's not going to die.

HELENE (jerking him away from cot):
    Don't touch him—

GERARD:
    Really, madame, Harry is very good at this sort of
    thing—

HELENE (scornfully):
    I've seen a sample of his work—and I wouldn't let
    him touch my dog!

MORGAN:
    I stopped the bleeding, didn't I? That was more than
    you could do.

HELENE (almost beside herself; to Gerard):
    Once and for all, are you going to get a doctor or do
    you want me to go and do it?

MORGAN:
    Go ahead.

GERARD:
    Madame, I've told you it is impossible.

HELENE:
> All right—I'll show you how impossible it is.

She starts for door, and Gerard stops her.

GERARD (pleading with her):
> Please, madame. Control yourself. It will mean ruin—not only for us all—but for our cause.

HELENE (scornfully):
> The cause! The cause! That's all you think of. Paul is nothing to you. Well, he is to me, and if I haven't got something to say about this thing I'd like to know who has? Who put up the money for all this? Where would you be if it wasn't for me?

And she struggles like a madwoman to release herself from Gerard's grasp.

GERARD:
> Madame! Please—I beg you—

HELENE:
> Let me go! I'm an American citizen—and I'm not afraid of anybody!

MORGAN:
> Why don't you sing "The Star-Spangled Banner"? (To Gerard.) Let her go, Frenchy.

GERARD: (amazedly):
> Let her go? You know what it means if she appears on the street?

MORGAN:
> She won't go anywhere. She's just sounding off.

He pulls Gerard away from Helene, who stands there and stares at him infuriatedly.

MORGAN:
> You see?][90]

Helene suddenly hits him in the face. Morgan grins at her and introduces her to Marie, who has entered at this juncture with pan containing probe he gave cashier to sterilize.

[MORGAN:
> Miss Browning, this is Madame de Cheesecake. (Taking pan from Marie, he says to Helene.) Don't get tough with Slim. She's apt to slap you back.

MARIE (to Helene):
> Is there something I can do?

HELENE (icily):
> Don't ask me. Your friend seems to be in complete charge here.

MARIE (looking toward ceiling):
> Listen.

OVERHEAD we HEAR Cricket softly beginning to play plink-plink prelude.

MORGAN (opening medical kit):
> What is it?

MARIE:
> I told Cricket to play that if Renard came in.

Morgan looks at Helene.

MORGAN (lowering voice):
> That's the Gestapo. (Taking out can of ether and a packet of cotton, he hands it to Helene.) Get over there behind your husband's head, and if he comes to while I'm probing, pour some of that stuff on a hunk of cotton and give him a whiff of it to keep him quiet. (To Gerard.) Bring that lamp over here so I can see.

HELENE (unscrewing stopper from can):
> What is this?

MORGAN (preparing to go to work with probe):
> Ether. Be careful you don't get too many whiffs of it yourself, Cheesecake.

HELENE (brandishing can in a frenzy):
> If you call me that again, I'll throw this can clear through you!

GERARD (in alarm):
> Hush!

MORGAN:
> You better save it for Mr. Cheesecake.

As Helene glares at him, speechless with rage, Marie reaches for can.

MARIE:
> I'll do it.

HELENE (haughtily):
> Are you a nurse?

MARIE:
> No. Are you?

HELENE:
> Yes. I took a course in Paris. That's why all this seems so horrible to me.

She goes and stands behind Paul, preparing to give ether to him if he needs it. Morgan looks at her and motions to Marie.

MORGAN:
> You better get out of here. You might not like this.

MARIE:
> I'll be all right.][91]

She picks up candle to give Morgan more light. Helene, watching Morgan shove probe into wound, suddenly keels over on the floor in a dead faint.

[MORGAN (seeing this):
    Look at our nurse.

MARIE (going to her aid):
    Oh, you poor thing.

MORGAN:
    Let her alone—and pick up that can—quick.

Marie obeys—but it is too late.

MARIE:
    It's all spilled.

MORGAN (in disgust):
    You dames! Pull Nursie away from it—and fan those
    ether fumes off me.

He continues to probe, and Paul, coming to, begins to
groan and writhe in agony. Gerard gazes fearfully at ceiling.

GERARD:
    You better stop.

MORGAN:
    I can't. (To Paul.) Take it easy. I'll be through in a
    minute. (To Gerard.) Put that lamp down. You and
    Slim'll have to hold him.

They obey, Marie gripping Paul's good arm, Gerard
clutching his legs. Paul's groans become louder and
louder. Helene dazedly sits up on floor.

MORGAN (to Marie):
    Put your hand over his mouth.

HELENE:
    Stop it. Stop it. Can't you see you're killing him?

MORGAN:
    It's your fault—spilling all the ether. See if you can
    find something for him to bite on. Then he won't
    make so much noise.

Helene looks toward ceiling, recalls Renard, rises, and goes around other side of bed. She evidently finds something for Paul to bite on, judging from muffled SOUND of his groans.

MORGAN (after a moment):
Here's the bullet.

He holds it up and Paul sinks back with a gasp of relief, his teeth relaxing their grip on the object Helene gave him to bite on. It was nothing less than the knuckle of the index finger of her own right hand, and blood is slowly welling up in the teeth marks.

MORGAN (seeing this):
Are you crazy?

HELENE:
It was my fault he was suffering so much. Why shouldn't I share it?

Marie, staring at Helene, makes a sudden rush for the bathroom, her hand clutching mouth.

MORGAN:
You dames! If it isn't one thing it's the other.

Then, as he starts to put bandage on Paul's wound, we
DISSOLVE TO:]⁹²

50.   [INT. CELLAR ROOM   THREE OR FOUR HOURS LATER
By candlelight Morgan, weary with a long vigil, sits by cot, watching Paul. On opposite side of cot Helene sits in a chair, watching Morgan. Latter, feeling Paul's forehead, takes hold of his wrist for a moment, then, blowing out candle and rising to feet, he stretches luxuriously in morning sunlight from dingy window.

MORGAN:
Guess I'll get some sleep.

HELENE:
Is he worse?

MORGAN (shaking head):
> No. Fever's all gone and his pulse is coming back strong.

HELENE (her face lighting up):
> He's going to be all right? Are you sure?

MORGAN:
> I'm no doctor—but he looks pretty good to me.

Helene suddenly breaks down—her eyes fill with tears—and she walks out of room.][93]

51.   INT. CELLAR
[Helene enters, sits down on chair, and sobs brokenly. Morgan enters and looks down at her.

MORGAN:
> You better get some sleep yourself. You've had a pretty tough time.

HELENE (broken and incoherent):
> I didn't want to come with Paul. But our people made me. They said no man was much good if he left somebody behind. The fear is too much. But I did my best to get out of it. I said I'd be in the way, but that wasn't it. I was simply afraid. More afraid to go than I was to stay. But Paul wouldn't leave without me. I thought he was very brave. But now I know he was afraid, too.

MORGAN:
> Well, he didn't invent it.][94]

[HELENE:
> But we have so much to do, and so little to do it with. You must tell these people what we are. It is only fair. You have risked everything to bring us here.

MORGAN:
> Not me. I got paid for what I did.

153

HELENE:
> You got no pay for saving Paul. And I tried so hard
> to stop you. I did my best. If I had something in my
> hands I would have killed you.

MORGAN (impatiently):
> Quit that baby talk. You aren't sorry at all. Nobody
> is. You're just sorry you made such a mug of your-
> self.

Helene stares at him for a moment, then smiles at him
through her tears.

HELENE:
> You can't make me angry at you any more. I don't
> know why. You could do anything to me. I wouldn't
> care.

MORGAN (grinning at her):
> Of all the screwy dames— (After a moment.) What's
> your name?

HELENE:
> Helene. Yours is Harry, isn't it? Harry. I never knew
> anybody by that name.

MORGAN (holding out hand):
> Same here. Glad to meet you, Helene.

As she puts her hand in his, palm down, French fashion,
somebody speaks behind them.

MARIE'S VOICE:
> You're supposed to kiss it.]⁹⁵

They turn and see Marie standing behind them with a
tray of food in her hands.

[MARIE:
> I hate to break this up, but—

MORGAN:
> But what?

154

HELENE (in surprise):
 Oh, hello.

MARIE:
 Oh, *hello*. (To Morgan.) How's your patient? Or
 haven't you seen him lately?

MORGAN:
 Lay off Helene. She's okay. (Nodding in Paul's direction.) So is he.

HELENE (to Marie):
 I'm sorry I was so rude to you.

MARIE:
 I'll get over it. (Setting down tray.) Here's some
 breakfast for you.

MORGAN (turning to go):
 Listen, Helene, if anything goes wrong, don't be
 afraid to send for me.

HELENE:
 I won't. Thanks.][96]

Morgan starts toward stairway. Marie looks at Helene.
The two women measure each other. Then, without a
word, Marie turns and follows Morgan. And as Helene
looks after them, we

DISSOLVE TO:

51A.   INT. UPPER HALLWAY   A FEW MINUTES LATER
Morgan and Marie enter, but instead of going toward her
own door Marie waits beside Morgan while he unlocks
his door.

[MORGAN:
 Why don't you go to bed?

MARIE:
 I could use a drink.

MORGAN (opening door):
> You're out of luck. Eddy finished that bottle.

He walks into room, and Marie follows him.

MARIE:
> I didn't want one, anyway.][97]

51B.   INT. MORGAN'S SITTING ROOM
Morgan looking at Marie as she closes door.

[MORGAN:
> Is there something you want to talk about?

MARIE:
> No.

MORGAN (sitting down on couch):
> Well, I wish you'd get it over with as soon as you can. I'm dead for sleep.

MARIE:
> So am I. (Kneels down and takes off his shoes.) That feel better?

MORGAN:
> Nope.

Marie, rising, starts toward bedroom.

MORGAN:
> Where you going?

MARIE:
> Run a tub for you.

MORGAN (rising):
> No use. I'd only go to sleep in it.

MARIE (returning to him):
> Isn't there something I can do for you, Steve?

MORGAN:
> Yeah.

There is no mistaking his meaning, and Marie smiles at him.

MARIE (imitating Helene):
> You can't make me angry at you any more. I don't know why. You could do anything to me. I wouldn't care.

As Morgan looks at her she turns and starts toward door.

MORGAN:
> Wait a minute. (As she pauses he motions to her.) Come back here. (As Marie obeys.) Walk around me.

MARIE (puzzled):
> Huh?

MORGAN:
> Go ahead. Nobody's going to bite you.

Still puzzled, Marie slowly obeys. But by the time she has walked around him she isn't so puzzled.

MARIE:
> You're right, Harry. There's no strings tied to you. (Starting toward door.) I'm glad you brought it up.

MORGAN:
> It was getting me down.

He follows her to door, and as she opens it and goes out,]⁹⁸ [Gerard hurriedly enters.

MORGAN (seeing Gerard):
> What's the matter?

GERARD:
> Renard's downstairs. He wants to see you.

Morgan shakes his head.

MORGAN:
> I'm too woozy to talk to him now. Tell him I'm in bed—see him in the morning.

GERARD:

    Harry, you better come down. I think he suspects something.

MORGAN:

    Sure he does. That's why I don't want to talk to him.

MARIE (entering from hall):

    Take a cold shower. You'll be all right. (Starting toward bathroom.) I'll fix it.

MORGAN:

    Okay. (To Gerard.) Go down and entertain him.

GERARD:

    Eddy's doing that already.

MORGAN (in alarm):

    Eddy! Holy mackerel! (Sitting down and putting on shoes.) Never mind the shower, Slim.

He jumps up and exits into hall, followed by Gerard and Marie:][99]

[51C. INT. UPPER HALLWAY

Morgan, coming out of room with Marie and Gerard, says to Marie:

MORGAN:

    See you later.

MARIE:

    I'm going with you.

MORGAN:

    No, you're not.

He shoves her toward door of her room. Key is in the lock. Morgan opens door, pushes Marie inside in spite of her protests, and, locking door, starts down hall with Gerard.][100]

52.   INT. CAFE

Eddy sitting at table with Renard and Coyo. Bodyguard stands behind Renard. Place is deserted except for early morning help getting things ready to open up for business.

[EDDY (taking a drink):
    He must have weighed nine hundred if he weighed a pound. You never saw such a marlin in your born days.

Morgan, entering on stairway with Gerard, hurriedly comes down to table.

RENARD (seeing Morgan):
    Good morning, Captain. Won't you join us?

MORGAN (as he sits down):
    I don't seem to have much choice.

GERARD:
    Anything I can get you gentlemen?

RENARD:
    Not now.][101] (To Eddy.) Continue, Mr. Eddy.

Gerard goes about his business.

EDDY (beaming):
    Did you hear that, Harry? He called me Mister. (To Renard.) [Well, sir, this fish was so big Harry and me could hardly budge him. We pumped on him till we was all wore out. (Taking another drink.) Long after dark we was still playing him. He must have weighed a thousand easy.

RENARD (turning to Morgan):
    I'm glad you arrived. Every time Mr. Eddy takes a drink this fabulous fish grows larger.][102] How did you finally manage to land such a leviathan?

[MORGAN (pouring self a drink):
We had to cut him loose around eight o'clock.

RENARD:
Why? Was he so big?

MORGAN:
No.][103] We ran into a German submarine.

RENARD (startled):
A German submarine?

MORGAN:
Well, whatever it was, it turned a searchlight on us
and opened fire. [So I didn't stick around to make
any further inquiries.

Renard smiles admiringly.

RENARD:
You are very shrewd, Captain Morgan. I don't think
anybody could give a more logical explanation for refusing to obey the challenge of our patrol ship. Not
to speak of shooting out their searchlight.

MORGAN:
The patrol ship? Is that what it was? (Turning to
Eddy.) You were right, after all.][104]

EDDY:
I'm a good man in the dark. I always was.

[COYO:
There's one thing very hard to understand.

MORGAN:
What's that?

COYO:
Why a professional fisherman goes fishing for his
own amusement.

MORGAN:

I don't as a rule. But Johnson lost my heavy tackle, and I figured the fish that took it might be drowned if he couldn't get shut of it—so while I was trolling for the line I got hooked on to another one.

RENARD (looking at Coyo):

That seems reasonable. Quite reasonable. (Pouring drink.) Sorry to bother you, Captain.

MORGAN:

That's all right.

RENARD:

You are a very practical man, and I'm quite sure you have no special sympathies.

MORGAN:

That's right.][105]

[COYO:

There was only one possibility that might affect your judgment. (Pause.) Your financial condition.

MORGAN:

Why don't you do something about it?

RENARD:

That's one reason I came here. To rectify that mistake. (Taking large envelope out of pocket.) Here are the passports of yourself and mademoiselle. Eight hundred and twenty-five dollars in cash, representing your claim against the Johnson estate. And thirty-two dollars of your own money. (As Morgan stares at him, flabbergasted.) Will you see if it is correct and sign this receipt?

As Morgan hastily checks contents of envelope, Renard and Coyo rise to their feet.

MORGAN:

It's all here.

Coyo hands him fountain pen. Morgan signs receipt.

MORGAN:
Thanks a lot. There's just one thing.

RENARD (taking receipt):
You're quite free to do as you like. Stay or go. As you please.

So saying, he walks out, followed by his men. As they exit, Morgan picks up envelope and looks after them, deeply puzzled.][106] Frenchy enters from rear, beaming.

MORGAN:
Did you hear the same thing I did?

GERARD:
Most of it. [We did very well. It is clear they suspect nothing.

MORGAN (rising):
I'm not so sure of that.

He walks over and looks out crack in shade.

MORGAN:
That watchdog is still out there.

GERARD:
He always has been there. (Looking down at Eddy, who is dozing in chair.) That big fish of his was an inspiration. That and the German submarine.

EDDY (sitting up):
What fish?

GERARD:
I think it deserves a small libation.

MORGAN:
Wait till he sleeps this one off. (Pulling Eddy to his feet.) Go on back to the ship.

EDDY:
Okay, Harry. (Turns to go, then stops.) Say, Frenchy.

GERARD:
Yes, Eddy.

EDDY:
Did you ever know a fellow by the name of Juggins?

GERARD:
Juggins?

EDDY:
Who?

Gerard stares at Eddy bewilderedly, and Morgan grins as we][107]

FADE OUT

FADE IN

53.   INT. CAFE   THAT EVENING
Place is crowded. [Cricket doing "Hong Kong Blues" number.][108] Marie, standing by piano, sees Morgan coming in entrance from sidewalk. He looks around room and goes to bar.

MORGAN (to bartender):
Has Eddy been in?

BARTENDER (shaking head):
I haven't seen him, Captain.

Morgan comes over to Marie.

[MORGAN:
Hello, Slim. Are your things all packed?

MARIE (nodding):
Have a good sleep?

MORGAN:
Plenty. You look pretty good yourself. Seen Eddy around?

MARIE (shaking head):
> Wasn't he down at the ship?

MORGAN:
> No. Buy him something to eat if he comes in. I'll be
> back in a little while.

MARIE:
> Give her my love.

Morgan looks at her over shoulder as he exits behind
her.][109]

54.   INT. CELLAR ROOM
Paul is sitting up in bed. Helene is feeding him from tray
as Gerard looks on. They hear SOUND in other room and
Morgan enters.

MORGAN:
> Hello, folks. (To Paul.) How you feeling?

PAUL:
> Much better. [We are very grateful to you, Captain.

HELENE:
> More than grateful.

MORGAN:
> Forget it.

Morgan feels Paul's cheek and takes hold of his wrist.

MORGAN:
> You're doing fine. You ought to be able to get out of
> here tomorrow.

PAUL:
> We were just discussing that. I hear you're going to
> leave us.

MORGAN:
> I haven't gone yet.

PAUL:
You look for trouble?

MORGAN:
I don't know what to look for. This guy Renard has got me guessing.

GERARD:
I think you're wrong, Harry. Believe me.

MORGAN:
I hope so. (Turning to go.) Well, folks, if I don't see you again—

GERARD (stopping him):
Harry, before you go—please give us some advice.

PAUL:
No—no. We have bothered Captain Morgan enough.

GERARD:
But he knows about these things—much more than we. I think he has even fished in those waters.

MORGAN:
Where's that?

GERARD:
Off Venezuela. Around Devil's Island. Didn't you tell me?

MORGAN:
I been around there. What about it?][110]

[PAUL:
It is a long story. We have no right to trouble you with it.

HELENE:
It is not a long story. We came here to free a man from Devil's Island—a man who can do more than any other to free this island. It is quite simple.

MORGAN:

Yeah. Sounds very simple.

GERARD:

We are going to steal the patrol ship.

MORGAN:

Is that a fact?

GERARD:

Everything else has been arranged. We are not plan-
ning a jail break at Devil's Island. Nothing so foolish.
There is a high Vichy official there who has agreed to
simplify the whole matter of the escape.

MORGAN:

For France?

GERARD:

No. For five thousand dollars. Our ship merely needs
to enter the mouth of the river. There a boat containing the prisoner and the high official will come out to
meet us. Then we will exchange the money for the—

MORGAN:

Wait a minute. Where is this money? Or are you
going to steal that, too?

PAUL (smiling):

No. That is one thing that we have. We brought that
with us.

GERARD:

What d'you think, Harry?

MORGAN:

Listen, Frenchy, let's don't get in an argument.

HELENE:

You don't think we have a chance?

MORGAN (frankly):
    I don't know what to think. I never heard anything so crazy in my life. In the first place, how are you going to steal the patrol ship?

GERARD:
    We thought you might suggest something.

MORGAN:
    I can't. I never stole a patrol ship.

HELENE:
    We'll manage it somehow.

PAUL (smiling):
    Helene is like you, captain. She is not afraid. I sometimes wonder why they chose me for this mission. As you know, I am not a brave man. The contrary, rather. I am always frightened.

MORGAN:
    Who isn't?

PAUL:
    Yet when you meet danger you never think of anything except how you will circumvent it. Obviously, the gestures of failure do not exist for you. While I— I think always—"Suppose I fail?"][111]

[MORGAN:
    Are you thinking that now?

PAUL:
    Yes.

MORGAN:
    I don't blame you. (Holding out hand.) So long—and lots of luck. You're sure going to need it.

PAUL:
    Same to you, Captain. And thanks.

MORGAN (turning to Helene):
> Good-by. (As they shake hands.) I wish there was something I could do for you people.

HELENE (smiling):
> There's one thing.

MORGAN:
> What's that?

HELENE:
> Send us back some cooler weather. (Opening dress at throat.) Is it always so warm here?

She picks up fan and starts to use it.

MORGAN (examining texture of her frock):
> You'll die in this kind of stuff.

HELENE:
> It's all I have with me.

MORGAN:
> I'll have Slim get you something lighter.

He walks out. There is a moment of silence, which is broken by Gerard.

GERARD (glumly):
> Well, here we are.

HELENE:
> Are all Americans like this? Have they no feeling, no pity?

PAUL:
> They are hard to arouse, but once it is done, their anger is terrible.

GERARD:
> Harry has no feeling for anyone—except Eddy.][112]

CUT TO:

55.   INT. CAFE

[Marie sitting at table near piano and doing card tricks for Cricket and orchestra. Morgan, entering from behind bar, comes over to table, looking around room for Eddy.

MARIE:
    He hasn't come in yet.

MORGAN (worried):
    I'll break his neck.

MARIE:
    Maybe he went up to your room.

MORGAN:
    Yeah. I'll go up and see.

Marie raises deck and riffles it in front of him.

MARIE:
    Decide on some card.

MORGAN:
    Okay. (Leaning over her and lowering voice as she shuffles cards.) Go out and buy Helene a couple of light dresses and things.

MARIE (taking card out of his pocket):
    Is this the card?

MORGAN (grinning):
    Huh! You're pretty good.

MARIE:
    Going to take her along with us?

MORGAN (startled):
    Say, that's not a bad idea.

He starts out toward rear, presumably to see if Eddy is up in his quarters. Marie, picking up handbag, rises and starts toward street entrance.

CRICKET:
> Where you going?

MARIE (as she goes):
> Down the street a ways.][113]

56.   INT. MORGAN'S SITTING ROOM
Door opens and Morgan enters. As he turns on light he hears SOUND in bedroom. His face lights up.

[MORGAN:
> That you, Eddy?

HELENE'S VOICE (in bedroom):
>   No. It's me.

Amazed, Morgan walks over to half-open door.

MORGAN:
> What are you doing up here?

HELENE'S VOICE:
> Frenchy brought me up the back way.

MORGAN:
> What for?

HELENE'S VOICE:
> I'd like to take a bath—if you don't mind?

MORGAN:
> Why pick on me? Why didn't he put you in Slim's place?

HELENE'S VOICE:
> May I use your bathrobe?

MORGAN:
> Help yourself.

He walks over to table, lights a cigarette. Helene enters from bedroom, wearing his bathrobe.

HELENE:
I wanted to talk to you.

MORGAN:
It's no use. I wouldn't take that job if you offered me the whole five thousand.

HELENE:
We'll give you more than that when this island is free.

MORGAN:
I'm through working on the cuff. Once was enough. (Grins.) Now I'll make you a proposition.

HELENE:
I'd listen to anything.

MORGAN:
Slim and I are pulling out of here tonight. Why don't you come along with us?

HELENE (blankly):
What?

MORGAN:
You heard me.

HELENE:
You believe I would leave my husband?

MORGAN:
Nobody would blame you.

HELENE:
It's nice of you to feel sorry for me. I feel sorry for you, too.

MORGAN:
Why?

HELENE:
You look down so much upon Paul. You think you are so brave and that he is so weak. Well, I wouldn't

have him any other way. I wouldn't have him like
you if I could. I love him just the way he is, and I
shall never leave him, no matter what happens.

MORGAN (grinning at her):
Never?

HELENE:
Never.

MORGAN (kissing her):
Never be too sure.][114]

As she draws back and stares at him there is a SOUND of
running feet in hall. Then door is burst open and Marie
breathlessly rushes in. [She carries paper-wrapped parcel
in her hands.

MARIE (taking in tableau):
I hate to interrupt you two so much, but—

MORGAN:
But what?

MARIE:
Renard is on his way up here—

MORGAN (closing door):
Did he see you come up?

MARIE:
I don't think so.

Morgan points toward bedroom.

MORGAN:
Take her in there.

Marie grabs Helene's arm and starts toward bedroom.

MARIE (as she goes):
Better wipe off that rouge, Steve.

As they exit Morgan takes out handkerchief, wiping lips and going to hall door. He opens it and sees Renard approaching in hallway with Coyo and bodyguard.][115]

[MORGAN (affecting surprise):
   Hello, there.

RENARD:
   Hello, Captain.

MORGAN:
   You want to see me?

RENARD:
   Yes.

MORGAN:
   Let's go below. It's much cooler.

RENARD:
   Yes, but it is much more private here.

He walks in, his two henchmen bringing up the rear. Coyo closes door.

MORGAN:
   Well, what's on your mind?

Renard looks around, sniffs the air.

RENARD:
   Very nice perfume. Sorry if we interrupted you.

Morgan grins and turns toward bedroom.

MORGAN:
   Come on out, Slim.

In reply bedroom door opens and Marie enters.][116]

RENARD (seeing her):
   Well, now we are all here— [except Mr. Eddy.

MORGAN (after a moment):
   Humph! So that's where he is.

173

RENARD (seating himself):
> Yes. We picked him up shortly after he left here this morning.

MORGAN:
> What did he do?

RENARD:
> Nothing. But knowing your affection for him, we decided to make use of it.

MORGAN:
> Is that a fact?

He slowly starts toward Renard, but bodyguard blocks his path, putting hand under coat with a menacing gesture. Morgan pauses, and bodyguard, using free hand, motions Morgan to return to other side of table.

MORGAN:
> Don't you ever talk?

BODYGUARD:
> Not unless it is necessary.

RENARD:
> Please sit down over there, Captain.

He indicates chair on other side of table. Morgan, looking at bodyguard and measuring distance between them, thinks better of it and obeys Renard's injunction.

MORGAN (sitting down in chair):
> What are you going to do to Eddy?

RENARD:
> Well, your friend seems to be in a delicate condition, so instead of plying him with liquor and getting stories about a larger fish I have decided to withhold it for a while and see what happens.

MORGAN:
> You can't do that. You'll kill him.

RENARD:
> You should know.

MORGAN:
> He can't stand it. He'll go crackers.

RENARD:
> You can easily prevent it.

MORGAN:
> Yeah.

COYO (suddenly):
> Please put your hands on the table, Captain.][117]

Morgan looks at him, but makes no move to lift his hands, which are out of sight below level of table. Bodyguard starts forward, pulling revolver out from under coat. Morgan sees this, and as bodyguard aims weapon at him Morgan fires at him through compartment in table. Bodyguard, dropping gun and clutching stomach, falls face down on table. Marie screams at the shot, while Morgan, rising to his feet, gun in hand, throws it down on Renard and Coyo, both of whom sit as if paralyzed by the murderous suddenness of it all—until they both realize that Morgan is going to give them the same. For as the latter slowly rises to his feet, the hammer of the weapon also rises.

[RENARD:
> It won't do you any good to kill us. That won't save Mr. Eddy.

MARIE (getting up):
> That's right, Steve—

Morgan, trembling with ungovernable rage, shakes his head.

MORGAN:
> I don't care. They've pushed me around all I'm going to be pushed.

MARIE:
Wait, Steve—

MORGAN:
Don't get in front of them.

MARIE:
Steve! Listen to me!

MORGAN (shoving her toward door):
Go downstairs and tell Cricket to play real loud for a few minutes.

MARIE (in desperation):
Steve! Why don't you try to make a deal with them?

MORGAN:
Hurry up. Do what I tell you.

MARIE (turning to Renard):
Look—there's a phone out in the hall—

RENARD (coolly):
I know that, mademoiselle. But we have Mr. Eddy. If any deal is made, it will be made on our terms, not yours.

Morgan turns and looks at him.

MORGAN:
Is that a fact?

He starts toward Renard, gun in hand. Renard slowly rises to his feet. So does Coyo.

MORGAN:
You're going to tell me what to do, huh?

RENARD:
Yes.

MORGAN:
I guess you fellows have whipped a lot of people with rubber hose, haven't you?

RENARD:
> Yes, Captain.

MORGAN:
> Did you ever whip anybody with a pistol?

RENARD:
> No, Captain.

MORGAN:
> You must try it sometime—

And using trigger guard like a brass knuckle, he hits Renard in the stomach. As the latter doubles up and reels against the wall, Coyo makes a leap at Morgan, who hits him in the jaw. As he goes down, Renard pulls himself erect.

MORGAN (socking him again):
> All right—let's see which one of you boys is the toughest.][118]

DISSOLVE TO:

57.   INT. UPPER HALLWAY   A LITTLE LATER
[Coyo talking into wall telephone near doorway of Morgan's room. Morgan and Gerard watching him. Maybe Gerard is holding him up.

COYO:
> That's right. Let him go.

MORGAN (prompting him):
> We will explain later.

COYO (into phone):
> We will explain later.

As he hangs up, Marie sticks her head out of door.

MARIE:
> Renard's coming to.

Morgan, supporting Coyo, speaks to Gerard.

MORGAN:
>Make him fill out those passes we found in his pocket.][119]

58. INT. MORGAN'S SITTING ROOM
[Renard, dazedly lifting head from table, looks at Helene who has been pouring water from pitcher over his head. Morgan enters with Coyo, Gerard, and Marie, who closes door. Gerard puts passes in front of Renard and gives him fountain pen.

GERARD:
>Fill in the names of Harry Morgan, Marie Browning, and— (turning to Morgan, who is tying Coyo to chair) what's Eddy's first name?

MORGAN:
>Eddy. Eddy James.

GERARD (to Renard):
>Eddy James.

MORGAN:
>Make out one for Paul and Helene while you're at it.

GERARD:
>That's a good idea. (To Renard.) Paul de Bursac and Helene de Bursac.

. RENARD:
>Who are these people?

MORGAN (coming over):
>The two passengers I brought over from Anguilla. (As Renard stares at him, Morgan turns to Helene.) Go down and get your husband ready to travel.

HELENE:
>Where are we going?

MORGAN:
>Down to my ship for a starter.

HELENE (staring at him):
> You're going to do it?

MORGAN (tying Renard to chair):
> Not if you stand there gabbing all night.

HELENE (her eyes filling with tears):
> You'll never be sorry.

MORGAN (grinning):
> Never?

HELENE:
> Never.

She turns and goes out into hall, making exit to left to get over back way.

MARIE:
> Say, what is this? Where are you going?

MORGAN (gagging Renard):
> Get your bag out of your room. (To Gerard as Marie exits.) Give her a hand with it. And take along one of mine.

He points to two suitcases by door.

GERARD (indicating Renard and Coyo):
> What about them?

MORGAN:
> I'll talk to you about that downstairs.

GERARD:
> Okay, Harry. (Pausing by door.) Are you really going to take them to—?

He makes gesture toward south with head indicating Devil's Island.

MORGAN:
> Not if you can think of some better way.

Gerard smiles, tries to say something but chokes up, then goes and picks up both of Morgan's suitcases, looking at Morgan in dumb happiness as he starts out into hall.

MORGAN:
Don't strain yourself.

Gerard exits and Morgan carefully examines bonds and gags of his two captives.

MORGAN:
Well, boys, I guess that'll hold you for a while. (As Renard tries to say something through gag.) Be careful—you'll swallow it.

He turns and sees Marie standing in doorway, holding cigarette in her hand.

MORGAN:
All set?

MARIE:
Where are we going?

MORGAN (looking at Renard):
We're going to Devil's Island and get a man that'll set this place on fire. (To Marie.) Any objections?

MARIE:
What are you taking her for? What can she do?

MORGAN:
What can you do?

MARIE (after a moment):
Got a match?

Morgan, taking box out of table drawer, starts to toss it to her, pauses, opens box, and walks over to her, striking match and lighting her cigarette. As they stand there Eddy lurches up.][120]

EDDY (beaming):
Hello, Harry. How's everything?

[MORGAN:
  Fine. How are you?

EDDY:
  Fine. How are you?

MARIE:
  Fine. How are you?

Eddy looks at her and chuckles.

EDDY:
  Say, haven't I met this young lady before?][121]

MARIE:
  Was you ever bit by a dead bee?

EDDY (his face lighting up):
  Was you?

MARIE (nodding soberly):
  You've got to be careful of dead bees. If you step on
  them they can sting you just as bad as live ones.
  Expecially if they were kind of mad when they got
  killed. [I bet I've been bit a hundred times that way—

EDDY (delightedly):
  You have? (To Morgan.) You hear that, Harry? (To
  Marie.) Why don't you bite them back?][122]

MARIE:
  I would—only I haven't got a stinger—

Eddy looks at her a moment, rather puzzled.

[EDDY (feeling his forehead):
  I guess I better lay off for a while. I got a feeling I'm
  talking to myself. I never do that unless I'm pretty
  bad, do I, Harry?

MORGAN:
  That's right.

EDDY (feeling forehead and starting down hall):
  See you down at the ship.

MORGAN:

Okay. (As Eddy exits, Morgan looks after him and says to Marie.) You keep that up and we'll have that guy on the wagon in no time.

MARIE:

I'll do my best.

Morgan, taking key out of lock, prepares to go and waves to Renard and Coyo.

MORGAN:

Good-by, gentlemen. (As they try to say something through gags.) Same to you—and many of them.

As he closes the door and locks it from outside, we][123]

CUT TO:

59.   INT. CAFE

[Gerard waiting by bar. He sees Morgan entering with Marie in rear and goes to meet them as they come down stairway.

GERARD:

I sent your bags down to the ship.

MORGAN:

What about Paul and Helene?

GERARD:

I took them down there myself.

MORGAN (preparing to go):

Well, Frenchy, I'll be seeing you—

GERARD:

But, Harry—

MORGAN (to Marie):

Wait for me on the sidewalk, Slim.

MARIE:

So long, Frenchy.

Gerard nods at her mutely as she walks out.

Chilling: Joan Fontaine and Laurence Olivier in Rebecca

Yasmeen's plans.

irus: Q&A (HD) The the Covid-19 outbreak. **— Britain's Smallest** ID) A plane makes gency landing on ds beach.	**8.30 Coronavirus: Can Our NHS Cope?** **— Dispatches** (HD) Dr Saleyha Ahsan looks at questions about the health service, including bed capacity, the availablity of vital equipment and the protection of NHS workers.
HD) Andrew concocts take drastic measures. s' Choice.	**9.00 Putin: A Russian Spy Story** PICK (AD,HD) A look at Vladimir Putin's early years as President. See Critics' Choice.
) (Followed by Weather) **News** (HD) I by Weather) **yle — Football Fans** **eir Skin** (AD,HD) le looks at racism at football supporters.	**10.00 999: What's Your Emergency?** (AD,R,HD) With police numbers lower than they have been for decades, this edition looks at the increased demands on frontline police in Northamptonshire.
eir Skin (AD,R,HD) Part vo. Ian Wright charts the rise of black footballers through archive original interviews and a ion of individual stories.	**11.00 Emergency Helicopter Medics** (AD,R,HD) A woman tries to save her husband after he suffers a cardiac arrest, and a multi- vehicle collision in Bedford leaves one patient with potentially life-changing injuries.
Wrestling: Dynamite (HD) World (HD) **3.00** James French Adventure) The chef heads to ly. **3.50** ITV Nightscreen Judge Rinder (BSL,R,HD)	**12.05 Born to Be Different** (R,HD) **1.05** Coronavirus: Can You Avoid It? (BSL,R,HD) **2.00** Couples Come Dine with Me (R,HD) **2.55** Grand Designs (R,HD) **3.50** Coast vs Country (R,HD) **4.45** Location, Location, Location (R,HD) **5.40** Kirstie's Vintage Gems (R,HD) **5.50** Countdown (R,HD)

ewing ● **Generally suitable for all** ◆ **Caution recommended**

MORGAN:
What is it, Frenchy?

GERARD:
Those fellows up there—what shall I do with them?

MORGAN:
That's up to you, old boy.

GERARD:
Me?

MORGAN:
You've got to do something. They know where we're going.

GERARD:
Who told them?

MORGAN:
I told Slim in front of them. Accidentally on purpose.

GERARD (after a moment):
You don't leave me much choice.

MORGAN:
It's time you fellows started on the offensive, Frenchy. No fooling. (As Gerard stares at him, Morgan indicates orchestra.) All you got to do is to tell Cricket and the boys to play real loud for a few minutes.

Gerard nods dumbly and Morgan walks out front door and joins Marie. Gerard looks after them for a moment, and as they exit he pulls self together, walks across to Cricket, and speaks to him. Cricket nods, understanding, turns to orchestra, tells them what to play, then, setting crescendo tempo, we hear the music roar out full blast and see Gerard returning across room to go and do what he has to do.

FADE OUT][124]

THE END

Notes to the Screenplay

1 In the film, the Foreword reads, "Martinique, in the summer of 1940, shortly after the fall of France." The title that follows is "Fort de France."

2 None of this action is in the film. Throughout the screenplay I have used brackets to indicate changes in the film; the corresponding material is supplied in the Notes.

3 To indicate that Morgan and the quartermaster have been through this exchange several times before, Hawks rewrote this scene so that Morgan answers each question before it is asked.

MORGAN: Good morning.

QUARTERMASTER: Good morning, Capitaine Morgan. What can I do for you today?

MORGAN: Same thing as yesterday.

QUARTERMASTER: You and your client wish to make a temporary exit from the port?

MORGAN: That is right.

QUARTERMASTER: Name?

MORGAN (laughing): Harry Morgan.

QUARTERMASTER: Nationality?

MORGAN: Eskimo.

QUARTERMASTER: What?

MORGAN: American.

QUARTERMASTER: Name of ship?

MORGAN: *Queen Conch*, Key West, Florida. We're going fishing the same as we've been doing every day for over two weeks. We'll be back tonight and I don't think we'll go more than thirty miles off shore.

QUARTERMASTER: Five francs, please. One more thing. You will go nowhere near the vicinity of territorial waters, St. Lucy, or La Dominique.

MORGAN: Is that a new order?

QUARTERMASTER: Yes. The decree was issued last night by His Excellency, Admiral Robert, governor general of the French West Indies.

MORGAN: Oh! Good for him!

QUARTERMASTER: Why, any complaints?

MORGAN: No!

4 Eddy is asleep on the dock; Morgan douses him with a bucket of seawater.

EDDY: Oh, hello, Harry. How's everything? That feels good. Did you bring me a drink?

MORGAN: Horatio's bringin' it.

EDDY: You're my pal, Harry. I sure got 'em this mornin'.

MORGAN (laughing): You've got 'em every morning.

EDDY: Not last Thursday.

MORGAN: Oh, yeah. That's right, I forgot. You're right, Eddy. Oh, here's Horatio. Give 'im a hand, will yuh?

5 HORATIO: Good morning, mon capitaine.

MORGAN: Good morning. Did you get the bait?

HORATIO: Yes, sir. Plenty of it. That guard took a bottle of our beer.

6 EDDY: Harry, can I have—

MORGAN: Just one. [Enter Johnson, as described in script.]

JOHNSON: Good morning.

MORGAN: Good morning.

EDDY: Good morning, Mr. Johnson.

JOHNSON: Well, are we goin' out?

MORGAN: Well, that's up to you.

JOHNSON: What sort of a day'll it be?

MORGAN: Oh, I don't know. Just about like yesterday. Only better.

7 MORGAN: Yeah. Well, I'll need money for that.

This is a typical on-the-set line change. Hereafter, only the most significant changes will be annotated.

8 MORGAN: Let 'er go! Watch it, Johnson! There's your strike! Put on a little more drag. Not too much! You're gonna have to sock him. He's gonna jump, anyway! All right, hit 'im again now! Hit him three or four times! Stick it into him! Better get the other teaser in.

9 MORGAN: No, he's not! Ease up on that drag! Quick! If he wants to go, let 'im go!

JOHNSON: He's gone!

MORGAN: No, he's hooked good.

10 MORGAN: Reel 'im in!

JOHNSON: No. I'm sure he's gone.

MORGAN: I'll tell you when he's gone. Reel in fa—

11 Deleted.

12 JOHNSON: A dollar a day seems like an unnecessary expense to me.

MORGAN: He's necessary. Aren't you, Horatio?

HORATIO: I hope so!

EDDY: (Coughing.)

JOHNSON: Can't Eddy do it?

MORGAN: No, he can't.

EDDY: What's the matter?

MORGAN: He just lost a fish.

EDDY: Mr. Johnson, you're unlucky. Say, Harry, would it be all right
    if I, er—

MORGAN: In the icebox. Just take one.

EDDY: Thanks. Er—

13 JOHNSON: I was never bit by any kind of a bee.

EDDY: You sure?

JOHNSON: Yes, of course I'm sure.

14 Deleted.

15 MORGAN: Nothing. You just lost a rod and reel, that's all. You had
    the drag screwed down tight again and when the fish struck
    you couldn't hold it.

HORATIO: If you had the harness buckled down to the reel, that fish
    would have taken you along with him.

EDDY: You're just unlucky, Mr. Johnson. Now, maybe you're lucky
    with women. What do you say if we go out tonight?

16 JOHNSON: Fifteen!

MORGAN: You talk too much, Eddy.

EDDY: I know it, Harry.

MORGAN: Okay, forget it.

17 Again, the Pétain reference is deleted. As they leave the boat:

MORGAN: What about tomorrow?

JOHNSON: I don't think so. I, I'm fed up with this kind of fishing.

MORGAN: Well, I can see how you would be. Slack that off a little.
    You fish for sixteen days, hook into a couple o' fish that any
    good fisherman would give his life to tie into and lose 'em both.

EDDY: Er, Mr. Johnson, you're just unlucky. I never seen no one—

MORGAN: Shut up, Eddy!

JOHNSON: You said sixteen days. I only owe you for fifteen.

MORGAN: No. With today it's sixteen. And then there's the rod and
    reel.

JOHNSON: The tackle's your risk.

MORGAN: Not when you lose it the way you did.

JOHNSON: I've paid for the rent of it every day. The tackle's your risk, I tell yuh!

MORGAN: Look, if yuh hired a car and ran it over a cliff, you'd have to pay for it.

JOHNSON: Ah, that's different.

EDDY: Not if he was in it, Harry. That's a good one!

MORGAN: Yeah, that's good, Eddy. Now you lost the outfit through carelessness. It cost me two hundred and seventy-five. I won't charge you for the line because a fish that big could'a taken it all, anyway. And there's sixteen days at thirty-five a day, that's, er, five hundred and sixty. No, it's five hundred and sixty, Eddy. Now yuh got a little credit, so that'll be eight hundred and twenty-five altogether.

JOHNSON: Well—

MORGAN: That's what you owe me, and that's what I want.

JOHNSON: Well, I haven't got that much with me. I'll go to the bank in the morning. That be all right?

MORGAN: I guess it'll have to be.

JOHNSON: Well, let's go up and have a drink.

EDDY (laughing): That's a good idea.

MORGAN: You'd better stay here and lock up.

EDDY: Are you sure you don't—

MORGAN: No, Eddy.

JOHNSON: Look there! I thought everybody took their flag in after six o'clock.

MORGAN: Well, most of 'em do.

18 There are two civilians.

FIRST CIVILIAN: Suivez-le. ["Follow him."]

SECOND CIVILIAN: Entendu. ["Okay."]

19 FIRST CIVILIAN: Your names, please.

JOHNSON: Now look, we're Americans!

MORGAN: His name's Johnson. My name's Morgan. We're livin' over at the Marquis Hotel. That do yuh?

FIRST CIVILIAN: Merci beaucoup.

20 BARTENDER: Yes, sir?

MORGAN: What's yours?

JOHNSON: Bourbon.

MORGAN: Bourbon. And rum for me.

GERARD: Well, gentlemen, what luck today?

21 JOHNSON: Not me. I'm through. This is my last day.
GERARD: That's too bad.
MORGAN: Yeah.
JOHNSON: Here's to yuh! Well, I'm gonna clean up. Oh, that was eight hundred and, er—
MORGAN: —twenty-five.
JOHNSON: Eight twenty-five.
MORGAN: Uh-huh. Oh, Johnson!
JOHNSON: Yeah?
MORGAN: What time tomorrow morning?
JOHNSON: Oh, after I get to the bank. Say around ten-thirty, eleven o'clock.
MORGAN: I'll be waitin' for yuh.
GERARD: Any trouble, Harry?
MORGAN: No (laughing), no, Frenchy.
GERARD: Then you are free after today?
MORGAN: Yeah. Why?
GERARD: Er, there were some people in here today. They wanted to hire your boat.
22 MORGAN: Not a chance. Papa!
OLD MAN: Bon jour, monsieur.
CLERK: The key, monsieur.
MORGAN: Thank you.
GERARD: Please listen to me, Harry. They only want to use your boat for one night. They pay you well.
MORGAN: For what?
GERARD: Well—
MORGAN: I'd like to oblige you, Frenchy, but I can't afford to get mixed up in your local politics.
GERARD: I would not speak if it weren't important. I— Please, can I go with you to your room?
MORGAN: Sure. Come ahead.
23 MARIE: Anybody got a match?
24 MORGAN: Who's that?
GERARD: Oh, she came in this afternoon. The plane from the south.
MORGAN: Er, now look, Frenchy. Er, about that other thing. I know where you stand and what your sympathies are, and it's all right for you, but I don't want any part of it. They catch me foolin' around with you fellas and my goose'll be cooked.
GERARD: But—
MORGAN: Probably lose my boat, too. I ain't that interested.

GERARD: But they are coming to see you tonight.

MORGAN: Well, you better get word to them.

GERARD: Please—

MORGAN: Aw, they'd just be wastin' their time.

GERARD: Oh.

MORGAN: Sorry. I'll see yuh later.

25 Morgan lights a cigarette; he is sitting alone at a table. Marie leaves Johnson to stand by Cricket's piano and join him in "Am I Blue."

CRICKET: "Am I blue?
　Am I blue?
　Ain't these tears in my eyes tellin' you?
　Am I blue?
　You'd be, too,
　If each plan with your man done fell through.
　Was a time
　I was his only one,
　But now I'm the sad and lonely one,
　So lonely.
　Was I gay? 'til today—"

MARIE: (Humming.)

CRICKET: "Now he's gone and we're through,
　Am I blue?"
　Take over.
　"Was a time—"

MARIE: "I was his only one—"

CRICKET: "But now I'm—"

MARIE: "The sad and lonely one—"

CRICKET: "So lonely.
　Was I gay?"

MARIE: "Was I gay?"

CRICKET: "'til today—"

MARIE: "'til today—"

CRICKET: "Now she's gone and we're through, baby oh—"

MARIE AND CRICKET: "Am I blue?
　Am I blue?"

"AM I BLUE" © 1929 WARNER BROS. INC. Copyright Renewed. All Rights Reserved. Used by Permission.

GROUP (applauding, laughing): Bravo!

26 MORGAN: I didn't ask to see 'em. You better head 'em off.

27 MARIE: Hello.

MORGAN: Let's have it.

MARIE: What do you want?

MORGAN: Johnson's wallet.

MARIE: What?

MORGAN: Come on!

MARIE: What're you talking about? Say, mister, what's got into you? What do you think you're gonna do?

MORGAN: I'm gonna get that wallet, Slim.

MARIE: I'd rather you wouldn't call me Slim. I'm a little too skinny to take it kindly.

MORGAN: Quit the baby talk. Which is it?

MARIE: You know, Steve, I wouldn't put it past you. I didn't know you were a hotel detective.

28 MORGAN: Well, he's still my client. You ought to pick on somebody to steal from that doesn't owe me money.

MARIE: He dropped it and I picked it up.

29 MARIE: Besides, I need boat fare to get out of Martinique.

MORGAN: That's another good reason, but you'll have to get it from somebody else.

30 MARIE: Find anything?

MORGAN: Oh, about sixty odd dollars in cash and about fourteen hundred dollars in traveler's checks.

MARIE: Do you expect more?

MORGAN: That bird owed me eight hundred and twenty-five dollars. "I haven't got that much on me," he says. "I'll have to go to the bank and pay you off tomorrow," he says. And all the time he's got a reservation on a plane leaving tomorrow morning at daylight.

MARIE: So he was gonna skip out on you! Your client!

31 MORGAN: That's right. But if I hadn't stopped you, you'd'a gotten away with the whole works. After all, I am entitled to something. Don't you think so, Slim? What do you think's fair?

MARIE: I'll leave that to you.

MORGAN: Well, what would you say to—

32 MORGAN: Well!

GERARD: Please, Harry. I told them but they insisted on—

BEAUCLERC: It is not Gerard's fault, Mr. Morgan. Come in and close the door.

MORGAN: Well, you know, I told Frenchy I wasn't interested.

BEAUCLERC: I know. But close the door, please. I'm very sorry to intrude this way, Mr. Morgan, but this is a matter of great importance to us and we—

DE GAULLIST NO. 2: One moment.

MARIE: I'd better go. See yuh later.

MORGAN: Stick around. We're not through yet. It's all right to talk in front o' her, isn't it, Slim?

MARIE: Go ahead.

MORGAN: But it won't do you any good.

DE GAULLISTS: If you'd only listen—

MORGAN: It's no use. You boys are even takin' a chance coming here.

BEAUCLERC: We're not afraid.

MORGAN: Well, I am! I'm sorry, I can't do it and I won't do it.

33 DE GAULLIST NO. 2: It is more to us.

DE GAULLIST NO. 1: It is only a little voyage to a place about, er, forty kilometers from here.

34 DE GAULLIST NO. 2: That's all we have.

MORGAN: Well, boys, don't make me feel bad. I tell yuh true, I can't do it.

35 MORGAN: Yes, I know.

BEAUCLERC: Mr. Morgan, I thought all Americans were friendly to our side.

MORGAN: Well, that's right, they are. But you see there's a rumor going around that they put fellas on Devil's Island for doing what you're doing. I'm not that friendly to anybody.

BEAUCLERC: But they wouldn't do that to an American.

EDDY: Harry!

MORGAN: Do you really think that? Who's that?

EDDY: It's me, Harry.

MORGAN: It's all right.

36 MORGAN: Oh, hello, Eddy.

EDDY: Say, Harry, I wanted to talk to you about—

DE GAULLIST NO. 1: Mr. Morgan, could we continue—

EDDY: Who are these guys, Harry?

MORGAN: Eddy's a friend of mine.

EDDY: He was hangin' around the dock after yuh left.

BEAUCLERC: You've got a good memory for one who drinks.

37 EDDY: That's what Harry always says. But I ain't got no stinger!

DE GAULLIST NO. 1: Does he always talk so much?

MORGAN: Always. What do you want to see me about, Eddy?

EDDY: Er, oh, Harry, er—I guess I forgot.

MORGAN: That's all right. I'll, I'll see yuh down at the dock later on tonight.

EDDY: Say, Harry, could you— Thanks. You're all right. So long.

38 MORGAN: Sorry. Now look, boys, we could stay at this all night and the answer'd still be the same.

BEAUCLERC: Mr. Morgan—

MORGAN: I don't care who runs France or Martinique, or who wants to run it. You'll have to get somebody else. Come on, Slim. We still got some unfinished business.

MARIE: Good night.

MORGAN: Make yourselves at home, boys. Cigarettes on the table over there.

39 MORGAN: I want to see Johnson's face when you give it back to him.

MARIE: All right.

40 JOHNSON: I know. There's fourteen hundred dollars.

41 JOHNSON: Yeah. Sure.

MORGAN: Emil, yuh got a pen handy?

EMIL: Certainement, monsieur.

MORGAN: Eight hundred and twenty-five.

JOHNSON: Yeah.

42 MARIE: Say—

MORGAN: Stay where you are.

MARIE: I think I'm sitting on somebody's cigarette.

43 GERARD: Harry, this is awful.

MORGAN: Did they get 'em all?

GERARD: One got away at least. I think it was Beauclerc. Look, Harry, this is bad. But no one but me knows that you two saw them.

MORGAN: And Eddy, but he probably won't remember.

44 MORGAN: Frenchy, don't be a fool! Stay inside.

45 MORGAN: Cut it out, Cricket. He couldn't write any faster than he could duck. Another minute and these checks would have been good.

46 MORGAN: Who's that?

GERARD: Sûreté Nationale. ["National Police."]

MORGAN: Gestapo, huh?

GERARD: Uh-huh.

MORGAN: Lot of 'em, isn't there?

47 OFFICER: Yes, sir.

RENARD: Call attention.

MAN: Your attention, everyone!

RENARD: All this is regrettable, but there is no cause for alarm. We are only interested in those persons who have broken the rules laid down for their behavior. We shall pick out certain individuals. Those we do not designate will leave immediately. This place will then remain closed for tonight. This man. You. You. And mademoiselle.

48 Deleted.

49 COYO: That is all. You may go.
RENARD: Have you got all of them?
DETECTIVE: No, sir. Beauclerc and Emil got away.
RENARD: How?
DETECTIVE: They jumped off the wagon and went up an alley.
RENARD: Search all the places you have on your list.
DETECTIVE: Yes, sir.
RENARD: Continue.
COYO: And you, Capitaine Morgan, did you know these men?
MORGAN: No, I didn't.

50 MORGAN: Because he owed me eight hundred and twenty-five dollars.
RENARD: So at least you had no reason to kill him, did you?

51 RENARD: Mademoiselle. That is all for you.

52 MARIE: I arrived by plane this afternoon.

53 COYO: Why?
MARIE: To buy a new—hat. Read the label. Maybe you'll believe me then.

54 MARIE: I was—
MORGAN: You don't have to answer that stuff.
COYO: Shut up, you!
MORGAN: Don't answer it.
COYO: I told you to shut up!
MORGAN: Go ahead. slap me.

55 MORGAN: Well, you'll never do it by slapping people around. That's bad luck.
RENARD: Well, we shall see.

56 MORGAN: I don't need any advice about continuing to do it, either!
RENARD: Good night, capitaine.
MORGAN: Let's get out o' this.

57 Morgan and Marie are walking down the street; by the end of the scene, they are outside the Zombie cafe.
MARIE: Say, I don't understand all this. After all, I just got here.
MORGAN: Well, you landed right in the middle of a small war.
MARIE: What's it all about?
MORGAN: The boys we just left joined with Vichy. You know what that is?

MARIE: Vaguely.

MORGAN (laughing): Well, they got the Navy behind 'em. I think you saw that carrier in the harbor.

MARIE: Yeah.

MORGAN: Well, the other fellas, the ones they were shootin' at, they're the Free French. You know what they are?

MARIE: It's not getting any clearer.

MORGAN (laughing): Well, anyway, most of the people on the island, the natives, are patriots. They're for De Gaulle, but so far they haven't been able to do much about it.

MARIE: Oh.

EDDY: Harry! (Enters.) Are we in trouble?

MORGAN: No, Eddy.

EDDY: Well, I seen them guys pick yuh up and I was a-scared—

MORGAN: Well, everything's all right. You go on back and get some sleep.

EDDY: I'd'a got yuh out, Harry. (Hiccoughing.) You know me.

MORGAN: Yeah, I know you, Eddy. You go on back to the boat.

EDDY: Say, Harry, could yuh—

MORGAN: No.

EDDY: But—

MORGAN: No more tonight, Eddy. Beat it.

MARIE: I could use a drink myself.

MORGAN: Well, we can get one in here.

58 BARTENDER: What do you wish to drink, sir?

MORGAN: What'll it— (Laughing.) Er, we're, er, we're just lookin' around.

MARIE: Change your mind?

MORGAN: No money. Those guys cleaned me out.

MARIE: I forgot, too. Maybe I can do something. This has been a long day, and I'm thirsty.

MORGAN: Picked him out yet?

MARIE: You don't mind, do you?

MORGAN: If you're thirsty, go ahead. If I get tired o' waiting, I'll be back at that hotel.

MARIE: All right.

59 MORGAN: Come on in.

60 MORGAN: Yeah, that's right. I, I guess I did. You were pretty good at it, too.

61 MORGAN: Well, of all the screwy—

MARIE: All right. All right. I won't do it any more.

62 MARIE: I know you didn't. Don't worry. I'm not giving up anything

I care about. It's like shooting fish in a barrel, anyway. Men like
that. They're all a bunch of— I'm a fine one to talk. The pot
calling a kettle.

MORGAN: How long have you been away from home?

MARIE: This is about the time for it, isn't it?

MORGAN: Time for what?

MARIE: The story of my life. Where do you want me to begin?

MORGAN: I got a pretty fair idea already.

MARIE: Who told you?

MORGAN: You did. That slap in the face you took.

MARIE: Yeah? What about it?

MORGAN: Well, yuh hardly blinked an eye. It takes a lot o' practice
to be able to do that. Yeah, I know a lot about you, Slim.

MARIE: The next time I get slapped I'd better do something about it.

MORGAN: Hey, you forgot your drink.

MARIE: I don't want it.

MORGAN: Who's sore now?

MARIE: I am!

63 MORGAN: It's me.

MARIE: The door's unlocked.

MORGAN: Hey, you forgot your bottle.

MARIE: I said I didn't want it.

MORGAN: Hey, you are sore, aren't you? I asked you a question and
you didn't answer me. I said you're sore, aren't you?

MARIE: Look. I'm tired and I wanta get some sleep.

MORGAN: That's not a bad idea. What made you so mad?

MARIE: I've been mad ever since I met you.

MORGAN: Most people are.

MARIE: One look and you made up your mind just what you wanted
to think about me. You were— Oh, what's the use?

MORGAN: Well, go ahead. Keep on going.

MARIE: You don't know me, Steve. It doesn't work. I, I brought that
bottle up here to make you feel cheap. That didn't work either.
Instead, I'm the one who feels cheap. I've never felt that way
before. I wanted— I thought that maybe— Go on, get out of
here, will you, before I make a complete fool of myself?

MORGAN: How long have you been away from home, Slim?

MARIE: It's none of— About six months.

MORGAN: Goin' back?

MARIE: How?

MORGAN: What are you gonna do here?

MARIE: I don't know. Get a job, maybe.

MORGAN: Jobs are hard to get. I don't think you'd like it here anyway.

MARIE: Remind you of somebody, Steve?

MORGAN (muttering, laughing): This is brand new to me. I like it. Would you go back if you could?

MARIE: I'd walk, if it wasn't for all that water.

MORGAN: Yeah. Quit worryin', kid. You'll get back all right.

64 MORGAN: What the—

MARIE: Here's that bottle again.

MORGAN (laughing): Yeh. Well, it's gettin' to be quite a problem, isn't it? Do you want a drink?

MARIE: Nope.

MORGAN: I thought you were tired and goin' to bed.

MARIE: Yeh, I know. I thought so, too. You gave me something to think about. You said you might be able to help me.

MORGAN: That's right.

MARIE: Well, how can you do that if— Steve, you're gonna take that job with those men that were up here with Frenchy.

MORGAN: Yeah. If I can find what's left of 'em.

MARIE: I flew over Devil's Island. It doesn't look like such a high-class resort.

MORGAN: Yeh. That's what I heard.

MARIE: Well, I don't want to be the cause of—

MORGAN: Look. Don't you get the idea I'm doin' this just to help you. I need money, too.

MARIE: Won't Frenchy help you out without you having to do that?

MORGAN: I don't want his help.

MARIE: Don't do it, will you, Steve?

MORGAN: Look. Didn't you ask me—?

MARIE: Don't do it.

MORGAN: Why don't you take this bottle and go to bed?

MARIE (taking out money): Here. Can you use this?

MORGAN: I thought you said you were broke. You're good. You're awful good. "I'd walk home if it wasn't for all that water."

MARIE: Who was the girl, Steve?

MORGAN: Who was what girl?

MARIE: The one who left you with such a high opinion of women. She must have been quite a gal. You think I lied to you about this, don't you? Well, it just happens there's thirty-odd dollars here. Not enough for boat fare or any other kind of fare. It's

just enough to be able to say no if I feel like it. And you can
have it if you want it.

MORGAN: I'm sorry, Slim. But I still say you're awful good and I
wouldn't—

MARIE: Oh, I forgot. You wouldn't take anything from anybody,
would you?

MORGAN: That's right.

MARIE: You know, Steve, you're not very hard to figure. Only at
times. Sometimes I know exactly what you're going to say.
Most of the time. The other times— The other times you're just
a stinker. (Kisses him.)

MORGAN: What'd you do that for?

MARIE: I've been wondering whether I'd like it.

MORGAN: What's the decision?

MARIE: I don't know yet. (They kiss.) It's even better when you help.
Sure you won't change your mind about this?

MORGAN: Um-huh.

MARIE: This belongs to me and so do my lips. I don't see any difference.

MORGAN: Well I do.

MARIE: *Okay.* You know you don't have to act with me, Steve. You
don't have to say anything, and you don't have to do anything.
Not a thing. Oh, maybe, just whistle. You know how to whistle, don't you, Steve? You just put your lips together and blow.
(She exits.)

MORGAN: (Whistles.)

65 Deleted.

66 Like the preceding scenes, this one reveals not so much rewriting as
rearranging, with slight shifts in tone and emphasis.

COLORED WOMAN: It's all right. They have gone.

MORGAN: Go on.

BEAUCLERC: Well, you come along the lee shore of Anguilla from the
south. About three kilometers from the point.

MORGAN: There's a little cove and a jetty, isn't there?

BEAUCLERC: You know it, then.

MORGAN: Um-huh. The signals been arranged?

BEAUCLERC: Yes. Emil can show you.

MORGAN: Emil's not gonna be there.

BEAUCLERC: Please, Mr. Morgan.

GERARD: Why?

MORGAN: I'm doin' this my way.

GERARD: But we have—

MORGAN: I'm goin' alone. What are the signals?

BEAUCLERC: You flash a light to the shore. They will answer it with two lights. One held above the other. There will be two people to bring back.

MORGAN: How will I know 'em?

BEAUCLERC: We've never seen them.

GERARD: We know the name of one only. Paul de Bursac.

MORGAN: Well, that's good enough. How about landing 'em back here?

BEAUCLERC: Do you know Cape St. Pierre?

MORGAN: Uh-huh.

BEAUCLERC: A boat can meet you offshore there.

MORGAN: You be on that boat, Frenchy. I'll get out o' here around noon. Supposedly fishing. With a little luck and no patrol boats, I'll be back and off St. Pierre about midnight.

GERARD: U'mm.

MORGAN: I won't be burning any lights, so keep a sharp lookout.

BEAUCLERC: One thing, Mr. Morgan. Last night you very definitely refused to have anything to do with us. Why have you changed your mind?

MORGAN: I need the money now. Last night I didn't.

BEAUCLERC: If you knew what this means to us—

MORGAN: I don't want to know.

BEAUCLERC: I'm glad you're on our side.

MORGAN: I'm not. I'm gettin' paid. Oh, and, er, by the way, I'd like that money now.

MRS. BEAUCLERC: Charles, if I were you I do not think that I would trust Mr. Morgan.

MORGAN: Did you have a doctor look at his leg?

MRS. BEAUCLERC: No. They are watching all doctors who are friendly to us.

MORGAN: Miss the bone?

MRS. BEAUCLERC: Well, as far as I can tell.

MORGAN: He's lucky. Who told you to put a pillow under it?

MRS. BEAUCLERC: Why not?

BEAUCLERC: It doesn't hurt so much that way.

MORGAN: Well, it'll have to hurt and you'll have to take it unless you want to take a chance of gangrene setting in. All right, I'll take that.

MRS. BEAUCLERC: Are you a doctor?

MORGAN: No. But I've handled quite a lot of gunshot wounds. You can trust me now.

GERARD: Good luck, Harry.

COLORED WOMAN: It's all right.

67 The revisions in this scene make it clear that most of Hoagy Carmichael's contributions were worked out on the set rather than in Faulkner's draft of the script. It's also interesting to see how Marie's drinking (the rum swizzles that are prominent in each draft of the script, and her play with Eddy's "just enough to fill a hen's ear") is written out, along with some of her ironic tone.

WAITRESS: More coffee, mademoiselle?

MARIE: Please. What is that you're playing?

CRICKET: Did you say something?

MARIE: Yeh. What is the name of that tune?

CRICKET: It hasn't got any name yet. I've just been foolin' around with the lyrics. They're not so hot, either. Would you like to hear it?

MARIE: Sure. (Hums.)

CRICKET: "I run to the telephone whenever it rings;
   I can't be alone, it's one of those things;
   I tell a star my little woes,
   Hang around at a bar till it's ready to close."
   So it goes. And that's about as far as it goes.

MARIE: I like it.

CRICKET: Yes. If I could get the right lyrics.

MORGAN: Good morning, Cricket.

CRICKET: 'Morning, Harry.

MARIE: Hello, Steve.

MORGAN: How'd you sleep?

MARIE: The best in a long time. Have some coffee?

MORGAN: No, thinks. I've had mine.

MARIE: You were up early. What were you doing?

MORGAN: I was gettin' you a ticket on the plane this afternoon. It leaves at four. Can you make it?

MARIE: Sure. You took that job, didn't you?

MORGAN: Uh-huh. Yuh see, I figured this way you wouldn't get your feet wet.

MARIE: Yeah, that's right.

MORGAN: Well, that's what you wanted, wasn't it?

MARIE: Sure. I just— You want me to go, don't you?

MORGAN: Yes, I want you to go.

MARIE: Okay, Steve.

MORGAN: Help her get on that plane, will yuh, Cricket?

CRICKET: I sure will, Harry.

MORGAN: Well, I'm gonna be pretty busy from now on so I probably won't see yuh again. If I ever get up your way—

MARIE: Yeah. Do that. I'll leave my address with Frenchy so you can find me.

MORGAN (laughing): Maybe I'll know how to whistle by then. So long, Slim.

MARIE: So long, Steve. Well, it was nice while it lasted.

CRICKET: Maybe it's better this way, Slim.

MARIE: I don't know.

CRICKET: You haven't known him very long. He's a funny guy.

MARIE: Yeah.

68 EDDY: Oh (laughing) yuh can't fool me, Harry. I knew it just as plain. Say, could I have a little—

MORGAN: You're not goin'.

69 Deleted.

70 Deleted.

71 MORGAN: Say, Eddy—

EDDY: Huh. Thanks, Harry. I knew you was my pal. But why won't yuh carry me?

MORGAN: Because I don't want yuh.

72 EDDY: It's only me, Harry, it's only me.

MORGAN: How'd you get back on board?

EDDY: Oh, I, I went up the street and got a coupla bottles and then I sneaked in up fo'ward while you was workin' on the engine. I knew you'd carry me, Harry.

MORGAN: Carry yuh, nothin'. If I thought you could swim back I'd dump you overboard.

EDDY: Oh (laughing) you're an old joker. You and me's got to stick together when we're in trouble.

MORGAN: How do you know I'm in trouble?

EDDY: Oh, you can't fool me. I always know. Er, er, where we goin', Harry?

MORGAN: Eddy, what would you do if somebody shot at you?

EDDY: Shot at me? With a gun? (Laughing.) Who's gonna shoot at me?

MORGAN: If you're lucky, nobody!

EDDY: Er, now, Harry, er, where we goin'? What're we gonna do?

MORGAN: I'll tell you when the time comes. For now, get out some fishing tackle.

EDDY: Er—

MORGAN: Aren't you glad you came?

EDDY: No!

MORGAN: Here you are, Eddy, put this on. It's gettin' cold.

EDDY: I'm all right, Harry. Say, what's goin' on? What's the matter?

MORGAN: Nothin'.

EDDY: Yes there is, too. Well, what's all the darn guns fer?

MORGAN: In case we run into a shark or somethin'.

EDDY: A shark? At night? (Laughing.) "Or somethin'"? What do you mean "or somethin'"?

MORGAN: Watch your course, Eddy.

EDDY: What's the matter?

MORGAN: We're goin' on a job. I'll tell you what to do when it's time.

EDDY: A job? What kind of a job? What do you expect me to do?

MORGAN: Do you know how to handle one of these?

EDDY: Of course I know how to handle one! Everybody knows how to handle a gun. All you do is work the lever and pull the trigger. You know I know that. (Mutters.) Foolish questions. Do I know how to handle a gun! (Mutters.) What I gotta work a gun for?

MORGAN: Oh, I just wondered if you could.

EDDY: You know I can. Harry, sometimes you act stupid. Just plain stupid. Sometimes I think you don't pay no attention to nothin' I say. Sometime— Is it gonna be that bad, Harry?

MORGAN: I don't know yet. It all depends on how lucky we are.

EDDY: Oh. That's why you didn't want to carry me. I knew there was some other reason. You wasn't mad at me at all. You was afraid I'd get hurt! You was thinkin' o' me!

MORGAN: Watch your course, Eddy.

EDDY (laughing): I feel better now, Harry. I'll be all right. You'll see. What's the matter, Harry? What're you lookin' at me like that fer?

MORGAN: (Laughing.)

EDDY: What're you laughin' at?

MORGAN: Just a joke that neither one of us knows the answer to.

EDDY: What joke?

MORGAN: Whether you're gonna hold together or not. (Laughing.)

EDDY: Don't say that, Harry. I'm a good man! You know I am.

MORGAN: Yeah, I know you are, but you're goin' all over the ocean. Stay on your course.

EDDY: Oh, why do you always— Say, Harry, could I have just one? I don't want to get the shakes.

MORGAN: Well, make it a short one. I want you rum-brave, but I don't want you useless.

EDDY: Thanks, Harry.

73 Deleted.

74 Deleted.

75 EDDY: What's the matter, Harry? Who's that? What're we goin' to do?

MORGAN: We're gonna pick up a couple o' guys. Here's what I want you to do. Take this gun and get back there in the stern. If there's any trouble, start shootin', but don't shoot me.

EDDY: Yeah, but supposin' somethin' happens to you. What do I do then?

MORGAN: How do I know? You invited yourself on this trip. Not me. All right, get back there.

76 MORGAN: My name's Harry Morgan. Beauclerc sent me. Get that light out o' my face.

GUIDE: ["They've sent an American!"]

PAUL: What happened to Beauclerc?

MORGAN: Well, he ran into a little trouble. What's your name?

PAUL: De Bursac.

MORGAN: That's the name. It's all right, Eddy. Come on aboard. Hey, wait a minute. He didn't say anything about a woman.

PAUL: Permit me, captain. This is my wife, Madame de Bursac.

HELENE AND MORGAN: How do you do.

MORGAN: What do yuh want to bring a— Well, it's your funeral. All right, let's get out o' here.

GUIDE: Vos bagages, s'il vous plaît. ["Your bags, please."]

77 MORGAN: It's all right, Eddy. You can relax now. And don't unload. We're not home yet.

PAUL: Mr. Morgan—

MORGAN: If she gets cold, you can put her down in the cabin.

PAUL: Mr. Morgan, just who are you?

MORGAN: I own this boat. Beauclerc's paying me to get you people back to Martinique.

PAUL: You're not one of us.

203

MORGAN: No.

PAUL: You're not on our side.

MORGAN: Nope.

PAUL: I don't understand.

MORGAN: I don't understand what kind of a war you guys are fightin', luggin' your wives around with yuh. Don't you get enough of them at home?

PAUL: But I don't—

HELENE: Mr. Morgan! You say you're being paid for this.

MORGAN: That's right.

HELENE: Then I suggest you stop talking and take us to Martinique.

MORGAN: Well, that's where we're headin' right now.

78   EDDY: What's the matter, Harry?

MORGAN: Keep quiet. I thought I saw somethin' out there. Listen.

EDDY: (Hiccoughing.)

HELENE: What is it?

PAUL: I don't know.

MORGAN: Shut up! Hey, yuh hear that?

EDDY: I—is it the patrol boat?

MORGAN: Don't you know those engines? Sounds like she's off there. All right, stand by that wheel. Wait a minute! Gimme that gun.

79   EDDY: I can do it! Er, what do yuh want me to do?

MORGAN: Well, if we're lucky, nothing. If we're not, hook her up and get away from here fast.

80   PAUL: What does this mean, Mr. Morgan?

MORGAN: Trouble if they see us.

PAUL: What can we do?

MORGAN: You can't do anything. Just get down on the deck, flat, and stay there. Although I don't know what good it's gonna do yuh.

PAUL: You will try to resist them with that?

HELENE: Please don't.

MORGAN: Shut up, both of you! Get down on that deck, flat! You save France. I'm gonna save my boat. Hook her up, Eddy, and let's go.

81   PAUL: Don't shoot!

PATROL BOAT OFFICER: ["Fire!"]

HELENE: Paul!

MORGAN: Well, we got lucky again. Now you can ease her off and put her on a hundred and sixty and then get that first-aid kit. Well, that's not so bad. You wouldn't have gotten that if you hadn't been so anxious to give up.

HELENE: Please, help me get him up on the seat.

MORGAN: Leave him where he is. I don't want him bleedin' all over my cushion.

EDDY: Here yuh are, Harry.

MORGAN: Okay, Eddy. You can have a drink now.

EDDY: Thanks, Harry.

MORGAN: Here, help me off with his coat. Easy now, boy.

82 A *painter* is a hitching rope, usually at the bow.

MORGAN: All right, get ready. The men in that boat will take yuh on from here.

HELENE: But, I don't understand.

MORGAN: A bunch of people spent a lot o' time figurin' this thing out. They know more about it than we do. [Pause.] This is de Bursac. She's the other guy I was supposed to pick up. His wife.

GERARD: My name is Gerard.

PAUL: How do you do.

MORGAN: Easy with him. He's been shot up a little.

GERARD: Well, what happened?

MORGAN: We ran into a patrol boat. He'll tell you about it. I'll cruise around a little and give you a chance to get ashore. Good luck.

GERARD: Thanks.

83 MARIE (singing and humming): "—how true,
With a smile—
. . . so rare"

CASHIER: Bon soir. ["Good evening."]

MORGAN: 'Evening, mamma.

MARIE: "Her complexion fair,
A lady indeed beyond compare,
Lo, how wonderful—"

EDDY: I thought you said she pulled out.

MORGAN: I thought she did.

MARIE: "She's an angel, too;
By the stars above
She's the one that I—"
Hello, Steve.

MORGAN: I thought you were gonna put her on the plane.

CRICKET: Well, Harry, she said—

MORGAN: What's the matter, didn't it go?

MARIE: Yes, it went, but I decided not to.

MORGAN: Oh, you did? You know, I went to a lot o' trouble to get you out o' here.

84 From this point on, Frenchy/Gerard's speeches were labeled FRENCHY in the script. I have changed the name to GERARD for consistency; no changes have been made in the dialogue.

MORGAN: Yeah. You dames! A guy goes out and breaks his neck to— Well, I might have expected it.

MARIE: Steve! You're not sore, are you?

MORGAN: Look, it would be all right if I had any dough, but—

MARIE: I got a refund on that ticket. Here.

MORGAN: Yeah. That's gonna help a lot. You'd better hang on to it.

EDDY: Harry, we can use—

MORGAN: She'll buy it for you. Nothin' but beer for him, Slim.

MARIE: I'll remember. We'll be all right, Steve. I've got a job.

MORGAN: Doin' what?

MARIE: Frenchy seems to think I can sing.

MORGAN: Well, it's his place.

MARIE: Sometimes you make me so mad I could—

GERARD: Harry!

MORGAN: You could do what?

MARIE: I could—

GERARD: Harry, I need your help.

MORGAN: Well, what is it now?

GERARD: That—

MORGAN: That's all right. Go ahead.

GERARD: That man is very badly wounded, Harry.

85 Deleted.

86 MORGAN: Me? I'm hotter than any doctor right now. Don't you think they recognized my boat? They'll be on my tail any minute. All I gotta do is walk out o' here.

GERARD: You don't have to go out.

MORGAN: You didn't bring 'em here?

GERARD: In the cellar.

MORGAN: Why didn't yuh put 'em on the center table in a goldfish bowl and be done with it?

GERARD: We had to do something. They're watching every road out of town.

87 GERARD: Please, Harry, will you do it?

MORGAN: Not a chance, Frenchy.

CASHIER: Captain Morgan, your bill here at the hotel, being overdue, amounts to six thousand three hundred and fifty-six francs.

EDDY: Six!

MORGAN: Well, she's right, Eddy. Well, you really keep the books, don't you, mamma?

CASHIER: We will be glad to dismiss the whole matter if you will do this for us.

88 MORGAN (laughing): You know, you almost had me figured right, mamma, except for one thing. I'll still owe you that bill. Now look, Slim, up in my room you'll find a medical kit. It's gray, and about this big with the name of the boat on it. Bring it down to the cellar.

MARIE: Sure.

MORGAN: Oh, and Slim! Here's the key. Bring some hot water, too.

GERARD: This way, Harry.

EDDY: Harry! Harry! Can I help?

MORGAN: No, Eddy. You just stay out o' sight. But if you should run across the police, don't forget what I told yuh to tell 'em.

EDDY: Er, what was that, Harry?

MORGAN: Uh—just stay out o' sight, Eddy.

EDDY: I remember.

89 Deleted.

90 MORGAN: Well, I'll tell you, I was sort of invited. He asked me.

HELENE: You're not a doctor.

MORGAN: No.

HELENE: Where is the doctor?

GERARD: Please, be patient, madame.

HELENE: I have been patient. How do I know you know anything?

MORGAN: You don't.

HELENE: Wait a minute.

PAUL: (Moaning.)

MORGAN: How long has he been unconscious?

HELENE: Just a few minutes.

MORGAN: Say, now, look, um— Well, he's got some fever and his pulse is a little low. He'll be all right, though, as soon as we get the bullet out of him.

HELENE: You're not to touch him. Do you hear?

MORGAN: That's all right with me. I'm not gettin' paid.

GERARD: Please! She does not know what she's saying. She's not herself.

MORGAN: Who is she?

GERARD: Harry, you promised.

MORGAN: Look. You want to help your husband, don't you?

HELENE: Yes.

MORGAN: Then use your head. They can't get a doctor without givin' the whole show away. Besides, he's probably got as good a chance with me as anybody.

HELENE: I'm not gonna let you do it!

MORGAN: Why not? He's no different from anybody else. Just a little sicker, that's all. It means he's not worth so much. Now, look—

91 MORGAN: You can have another crack at me later on. Hello, Slim!

MARIE: Hello!

MORGAN: Miss Browning, Madame de Bursac. Don't get tough with Slim. She's apt to slap you back. That's what you said you'd do, wasn't it? Bring the water in here.

HELENE: Wait a minute, I—

MARIE: He's only trying to help you.

HELENE: Who are you?

MARIE: Nobody. Just another volunteer. Where do you want this water?

MORGAN: In that basin. Is it hot?

MARIE: Boiling.

MORGAN: All right, then pour some of this in it. And drop these in. You'd better get out o' here. You may not like this.

MARIE: I'll be all right.

MORGAN: All right. Then take this.

HELENE: What is it?

MORGAN: Chloroform. Get over there by your husband's head and if he comes to while I'm probing, pour some of that stuff on a hunk o' cotton and give him a whiff of it. Don't open it till I tell you to. Take out about four of those. Oh, George, bring that lamp a little closer so I can see what I'm doin'. That's good. All right, Slim. Hold that a minute.

PAUL: (Moaning.)

MORGAN: Easy, boy.

PAUL: (Moaning louder.)

MORGAN: Come on. Hurry up!

92 MORGAN: Well, that's fine! Don't worry about her. Pick up that can. Any of it left?

MARIE: I think there's enough.

MORGAN: No, wait a minute. I don't think we'll need it. He's out, too. Bring that light down a little lower. Frenchy, bring that basin over here. And fan some of those fumes away, will you, or we'll all be out. There yuh are, Frenchy. There's your bullet. I told you it was spent. It would have smashed the bone. All right, I don't need that. All right. You finish bandaging it up. Adhesive tape in the box. I gotta get Nursie out o' here or she never will come to.

93 In place of this scene, whose dialogue shows up later, Hawks has Morgan carry the unconscious Helene into the outer room.

MARIE: What are you trying to do, guess her weight?

MORGAN: She's heftier than you think. You'd better loosen her clothes.

MARIE: You've been doing all right. Uh, maybe you'd better look after her husband.

MORGAN: He's not gonna run out on me.

MARIE: Neither is she. Steve! Is it all right if I give her a little whiff of this?

MORGAN: (Laughing.)

94 PAUL: (Moaning.)

MORGAN: Oh, you're with us again. You were lucky. You passed out.

PAUL: What happened? I must—

MORGAN: We'll talk about that in the morning. See if you can get some sleep.

PAUL: Thanks.

[Some time later:]

MORGAN: Why did you ever come along with him on a trip like this?

HELENE: I loved him. Wanted to be with him.

MORGAN: That's a reason.

HELENE: There's another reason. They told me to come. Our people did. They said—they said no man was much good if he left someone behind in France for the Germans to find and hold.

MORGAN: Makes sense.

HELENE: I told them I'd only be in the way, that I could do no good, that I was afraid. But the worst of it is that it's been so hard for him to have me along, because I've made him that way, too. Now he's afraid.

MORGAN: Well, he didn't invent it.

HELENE: Invent what?

MORGAN: Being afraid.

HELENE: Thanks, Mr. Morgan.

95 Some time later:

MORGAN: Well, the fever's gone.

HELENE: Do you, do you—

MORGAN: I'm no doctor, but he looks pretty good to me. If he wakes up, give him another one of these pills.

[In the outer room:]

HELENE: Mr. Morgan. Mr. Morgan— I—

MORGAN: You're not going to faint again?

HELENE: No. I'm just having a, a hard time trying to say something.

MORGAN: Well, go ahead. Say it. I'm not gonna bite yuh.

HELENE: Well, if it hadn't been for you, Paul might have— I'm sorry for the way I've acted.

MORGAN: Aw, you're not sorry at all. You're just sorry you made a fool of yourself.

HELENE (laughing): I have, haven't I?

MORGAN: Uh-huh.

HELENE: You don't make me angry when you say that. I don't think I'll ever be angry again with anything you say.

MORGAN: Another screwy dame. Now, how can you—

96 MARIE: Hello. I hate to break this up, but I've brought some breakfast.

HELENE: Good morning.

MARIE: How's your patient?

MORGAN: Oh, he'll be all right—

MARIE: Or haven't you looked lately?

MORGAN: He'll be all right. I'll be back this evening. If you need me before then be sure to call me.

HELENE: I will.

MARIE: Yes. And I hope you have everything you need here. The eggs may be a little hard-boiled—

HELENE: Oh, that's all right. I like them that way.

MARIE: You're lucky. Isn't she?

97 MORGAN: I'm gonna get some sleep. I'll see you later.

MARIE: Thanks.

MORGAN: What do you want?

MARIE: I can use a match. Thanks. Now I need a cigarette.

98 MARIE: Here, I can do that.

MORGAN: No.

MARIE: Oh, come on, let me help.

MORGAN: Look, when I get ready to take my shoes off, I'll take 'em off myself.

MARIE: All right. Want something to eat?

MORGAN: No.

MARIE: Just a little breakfast?

MORGAN: All I want to do is get some sleep.

MARIE: It's a good idea. I can help you there.

MORGAN: Hey, now where you goin'?

MARIE: I'm going to fix you a nice hot bath. It'll make you—sleep better.

MORGAN: Look, Junior. I don't want you to take my shoes off. I don't want you to get me any breakfast. I don't want you to draw me a nice hot bath. I don't want you to—

MARIE: Isn't there anything I can do, Steve?

MORGAN: Yes. Get the—

MARIE: "You know, Mr. Morgan, you don't make me angry when you say that. I don't think I'll ever be angry again at anything you say." How'm I doing, Steve? Does it work the second time?

MORGAN: You've been wantin' to do somethin' for me, haven't yuh?

MARIE: Uh-huh.

MORGAN: Uh-huh. Walk around me. Well, go ahead, walk around me. Clear around.

MARIE: (Laughing.)

MORGAN: Yuh find anything?

MARIE: No. No, Steve. There are no strings tied to you—not yet. (They kiss.) Oh, I like that. Except, except for the beard. Why don't you shave and we'll (light slap) we'll try it again.

99 GERARD: Harry!

MORGAN: Oh, later, Frenchy.

GERARD: No, Harry, wait! Renard, the inspector, is downstairs. You'd better come down.

MORGAN: Oh, I can't do that. I gotta get a shave.

GERARD: He's got Eddy!

MORGAN: He's got—

GERARD: Eddy! He's giving him drinks and asking him questions.

MORGAN: I was afraid o' that. Good thing you didn't get me in that tub!

MARIE: Look out for those strings, Steve. You're liable to trip and break your neck.

GERARD: Strings? I didn't see any strings.

MARIE: They just don't show, Frenchy.

100 Deleted.

101 EDDY: You oughta seen that fish. It musta weighed nine hundred if
     it weighed a pound. It was the biggest marlin you ever seen in
     all your born days. You know, a marlin is a swordfish.
     RENARD: Good morning, capitaine.
     EDDY: Oh. Hello, Harry. How's everything?
     MORGAN: Fine.
     RENARD: Won't you join us?
     MORGAN: A little early for this kind of a party, isn't it?

102 EDDY: Say, you're all right. Was you ever bit by a dead bee—
     MORGAN: No, he never was, Eddy. Go on with what you were
     sayin'.
     EDDY: Oh, I was just tellin' 'im about the big one we hooked onto
     last night.
     MORGAN: Uh-huh.
     EDDY: Well, sir, that fish was so big that me and Harry could hardly
     budge 'im. We pumped on him until we was all wore out,
     didn't we, Harry?
     MORGAN: Right, Eddy.
     EDDY (laughing): I—it was after dark and we was still playin' 'im.
     He musta weighed at least a—a thousand easy.
     RENARD: Every time Mr. Eddy takes a drink this fabulous fish grows
     larger.
     MORGAN: He must have started with a pretty small one.

103 MORGAN: Well, we didn't. Didn't Eddy tell yuh?

104 MORGAN: I didn't stick around to find out.
     RENARD: I do not think—
     MORGAN: You know, you can't be too careful these days.
     RENARD: I do not think anybody could give a more logical explana-
     tion for refusing to obey the challenge of our patrol boat. Not
     to speak of shooting out their searchlight.
     MORGAN: Patrol boat?
     RENARD: Yes.
     MORGAN: Oh, that's what it was. You were right, Eddy.

105 MORGAN: You know, it's a funny thing; he kept sayin' it was a patrol
     boat all the time and I wouldn't believe him.
     COYO: There is one thing that is not—clear to me, Captain Morgan.
     MORGAN: Yeah? What's that?
     COYO: Why does a professional fisherman go fishing for his own
     amusement?

MORGAN: Well, uh— Hey, don't you ever ask any questions? Don't you ever talk? No, I, I guess you don't. What were you saying?

COYO: Does a professional fisherman go fishing for his own amusement?

MORGAN: Well, he does if he likes it. And we like it, don't we, Eddy?

EDDY: Yeah. You remember that night in Key West when we went—

RENARD: We do not seem to be getting anywhere.

EDDY: It was the Fourth of July and you sa—

RENARD: Mr. Eddy!

EDDY: I was only gonna tell him at Key West, the Fourth of July, three years ago, at eight o'clock! I got that in, Harry.

RENARD: What about your passenger?

MORGAN: It was seven o'clock, Eddy.

RENARD: What about your two passengers?

MORGAN: You oughtn't to burn up at him. You fed him the rum.

RENARD: What about your two passengers?

MORGAN: What passengers?

RENARD: The ones you brought over from Anguilla!

MORGAN: He was waitin' on the dock when we came in. How do yuh think I got 'em ashore, in my sleeves?

RENARD: You could have landed them a dozen places on our coast line.

MORGAN: That's right. I could've at that.

106 RENARD: Would five hundred dollars refresh your memory?

MORGAN: Oh, my memory's pretty good. For instance, I can remember that you're the guy who lifted my passport and all my money.

RENARD: Would your memory become any better if your passport and money were returned to you?

MORGAN: Does that include the eight hundred and twenty-five dollars Johnson owed me?

RENARD: Why not?

MORGAN: And the five hundred you just mentioned?

RENARD: You drive a hard bargain, Capitaine Morgan.

MORGAN: Well, that's no bargain. If these people are as important as you seem to think they are, they're gonna be pretty hard to find.

RENARD: Not for a man of your resourcefulness. Think it over and let me hear from you.

107 MORGAN: Bee-lips went away pretty mad. As soon as he cools off, though, he's gonna start thinkin'.

GERARD: He thinks now that you will turn them in.

MORGAN: Well, that's what you want him to think, isn't it?

GERARD: What will happen then?

MORGAN: He hasn't searched this hotel yet, has he?

GERARD: No, not yet.

MORGAN: Well, there's your answer. He doesn't want them. He wants the whole set-up.

GERARD: Then what shall we do?

MORGAN: It's not "we," it's "you," and you can't do anything until that fella downstairs gets strong enough to move. Until then, you're probably safe. Better get rid o' this.

GERARD: Yeah.

MORGAN: Oh, bring us some breakfast, will yuh, Frenchy?

GERARD: Sure. (Eddy mutters. Marie has come downstairs and joins them.)

MARIE: I thought you didn't want any breakfast.

MORGAN: I didn't, then. What were you sayin', Eddy?

EDDY: I, I've been figurin'. Them guys don't think that I'm wise, but they was tryin' to get me drunk. (Laughing.) They don't know me, do they, Harry? (Hiccoughing.)

MORGAN AND MARIE: (Laughing.)

EDDY: I think they're tryin' to find out somethin'. What do you suppose it is?

MORGAN: Well, don't you know?

EDDY: No. I ain't got no idea. (Hiccoughing.)

MORGAN: That's a good way to leave it. You know, you got the hiccoughs.

EDDY: Have I, Harry? (Hiccoughing.) Oh, yeah. I never noticed it.

MARIE: Don't you think you better take a drink of water?

EDDY: What, water?

MORGAN: That's a good idea, Slim.

EDDY: No. Oh, no, not that. (Hiccoughing.)

MARIE: It'll do you good.

EDDY: I'll be all right. (Hiccoughing.)

MORGAN: Hey, Eddy!

EDDY: Yeah, Harry? (Hiccoughing.)

MORGAN: Keep out o' sight and stay away from the police. They're not goin' to believe that story you told the second time.

EDDY: What story was that, Harry? (Hiccoughing.)

MORGAN: Er, keep out o' sight.

EDDY: (Hiccoughing.)

108 CRICKET: "It's the story of a very unfortunate colored man
Who got 'rested down in old Hong Kong.
He got twenty years' privilege taken away from him
When he kicked old Buddha's gong.
And now he's bobbin' the piano just to raise the price
Of a ticket to the land of the free;
Well, he say his home's in Frisco where they send the rice,
But it's really in Tennessee.
That's why he say,
'I need someone to love me,
Need somebody to carry me
Home to San Francisco
And bury my body there.
Oh, I need someone to lend me a fifty dollar bill
And then I'll leave Hong Kong far behind me
For happiness once again.
Won't someone believe
I've a yen to see that bay again;
But when I try to leave
Sweet loco man won't let me fly away.
I need someone to love me,
Need somebody to carry me
Home to San Francisco
And bury my body there.'"

109 MORGAN: Well!

MARIE: I'm going to work. Do you like it?

MORGAN: Well, you won't have to sing much in that outfit.

MARIE: You know, Steve, sometimes you make me—

MORGAN: That's why I do it. Haven't seen Eddy, have you?

MARIE: No, not since noon. Why?

MORGAN: He left the boat and he hasn't come back.

MARIE: Is, is there anything wrong?

MORGAN: I don't know. Say, don't look now, but over there by the
door at the second table, there's a guy with a mustache. I think

he's following me. Keep an eye on him, will yuh? I'm goin' downstairs.

CRICKET: Hey, Harry! Stick around a while. She's goin' to sing.

MORGAN: I'll be right back.

MARIE: Give her my love.

MORGAN: I'd give her my own if she had that on.

CRICKET: Here's the rest of the lyrics, Slim. How do yuh feel?

MARIE: Well, I could use a drink, Cricket.

CRICKET: Sure. Come on. Emil! What'll yuh have, Slim?

MARIE: Scotch and soda.

CRICKET: Same.

110 PAUL: I'm very grateful to you.

MORGAN: Aw, forget it. Let me have a look at this. Uh-huh. Well, there's no bleeding.

PAUL: No.

MORGAN: Does that hurt?

PAUL: Very little. My only trouble is when I'm eating. I'm awkward with my left hand.

MORGAN: Well, we'll see if we can't arrange to have you shot in the other arm next time. You won't need me any more. Frenchy, I'm pullin' out.

GERARD: When?

MORGAN: As soon as I find Eddy.

PAUL: Is your friend missing?

MORGAN: Yeah.

GERARD: What happened?

MORGAN: I don't know. He left the dock and hasn't been back since. He usually does what I tell him.

PAUL: I'm sorry if anything happened.

MORGAN: Well, I won't know that until I find him.

PAUL: Couldn't you leave him here?

MORGAN: I don't think Eddy'd like that. Now look, Frenchy, as soon as I'm gone, Renard's gonna move in and turn this place upside down, so you better start figurin' how and where you're gonna move him and quick!

PAUL: Wouldn't it be best if we went with you, captain?

MORGAN: Why do you want to go? I'm still tryin' to get out of the jam I got into bringin' yuh here. Just why'd you come here in the first place? I know why she came; she told me, but why did you?

111 PAUL: Did you ever hear of Pierre Villemars?
MORGAN: Pierre Villemars? Yeah. I read in a headline. He was quite a guy. The Vichy got him. He's dead, isn't he?
PAUL: No, no, no! He's on Devil's Island. They sent me here to get him, and to bring him back here to Martinique. He's a man whom people who are persecuted and oppressed will believe in and follow.
MORGAN: Well, just how are you gonna get him away?
PAUL: You don't think much of me, Captain Morgan. You are wondering why they have chosen me for this mission. I wonder, too. (Laughing.) As you know, I'm not a brave man. On the contrary, I'm always frightened. I wish I could borrow your nature for a while, captain. When you meet danger, you never think of anything except how you will circumvent it. The word "failure" does not even exist for you. While I, I think always "Suppose I fail?" And then I am frightened.
112 MORGAN: Yeah, I can easily see how it wouldn't take much courage to get a notorious patriot off Devil's Island, but, uh, just for professional reasons, I'd like to know how you're gonna do it.
PAUL: We will find a way. It might fail. And if it does and I am, I am still alive, I will try to pass on my information, my mission, to someone else. Perhaps to a better man, who does not fail. Because there is always someone else. That is the mistake the Germans always make with people they try to destroy. There will be always someone else.
MORGAN: Yeah.
PAUL: Originally, we planned to do everything from here. But then, because of my own clumsiness, it was impossible. And that's the reason we have to go with you.
MORGAN: Oh, I couldn't even get you on the dock. They got a man down there watching; there's one upstairs; they're all over the place. How would I get you through the streets?
PAUL: How will you go?
MORGAN: Well, they're watching me to find you. As long as I haven't got you along, I can at least get on the boat. There'll be a fog again and the tide'll turn a little after midnight. I can cut loose and drift out beyond the breakwater before I start my engines.
GERARD: But, Harry—
PAUL: Captain Morgan is right. This is not his fight yet. Some day I

hope it may be, because we could use him. You have done
enough for us already. Gerard told me of your refusing Renard's offer to give us up.

MORGAN: How do you know I won't do it yet?

PAUL: There are many things a man will do, but betrayal for a
price—is not one of yours.

MORGAN: Good luck.

PAUL: I hope you find your friend.

MORGAN: Thanks.

HELENE: Good-by. And—thanks!

MORGAN: Oh, uh, Frenchy, I got a few things I want to talk to you
about before I blow.

GERARD: Well, then I'll be up in a little while, Harry.

113 Instead of doing card tricks or shopping for Helene, Marie is getting
ready to sing.

MORGAN: Any sign of Eddy?

MARIE: Uh-uh. But your friend's still sitting at his table.

MORGAN: Yeh. I know.

MARIE: What's the matter, Steve?

MORGAN: I dunno. I got a hunch the whole thing's gonna blow up.
It's too quiet.

MARIE: What are you gonna do?

MORGAN: We're gonna pull out o' here tonight. Soon as I find Eddy.
We're leaving here for good. The three of us. Now wait a minute. I want you to know what you're gonna get into. It'll be
rough. I'm broke. If we do get out of here, it'll be with a coupla
hundred gallons of gas and a few francs. Just about enough to
get us to Port au Prince, maybe.

MARIE: I've never been there.

MORGAN: I don't know when you'll get back home. Could be a long
time.

MARIE: Could be forever. Or are you afraid of that? I'm hard to get,
Steve. All you have to do is ask me.

MORGAN: How long will it take you to pack? There's a lot o' people
around here; save it. We won't shove off till midnight. Go
ahead and go to work.

CRICKET: You all set, Slim?

MARIE: Sure. Don't make it sad, Cricket. I don't feel that way.

CRICKET: You don't look that way either. Let's go. Top note, boys.

MARIE: "Maybe it happens this way;
Maybe we really belong together

But after all,
How little we know.
Maybe it's just for a day;
Love is as changeable as the weather
And after all,
How little we know.
Who knows why an April breeze
Never remains?
Why stars in the trees
Hide when it rains?
Love comes along,
Casting a spell.
Will it sing you a song?
Will it say a farewell?
Who can tell?
Maybe you're meant to be mine;
Maybe I'm only supposed to stay in your arms awhile,
As *others* have done.
Is this what I've waited for?
Am I the one?
Oh, I hope in my heart that it's so
In spite of how little we know. "

GERARD: Harry! Madame de Bursac wants to see you.

MORGAN: Now look, Frenchy, that's all over.

GERARD: She's up in your room.

MORGAN: She— Why did you—

GERARD: Please, Harry. That's all I will ask. Thanks, Harry.

114   MORGAN: Look, now you shouldn't have come up here. It's too much of a chance. I told you downstairs I can't take you.

HELENE: I know. I didn't come up for that. You've already done too much for us. But there's just one other favor I'd like to ask. I want you to take these. (Puts jewels in his hand.) They were my grandmother's, and her mother's before that. She gave them to me when I got married. They're all I've got left. I want you to take them out of here with you and save them till we can—

MORGAN: Suppose they get me before I get out?

HELENE: Then throw them overboard. At least they won't have them.

MORGAN: Suppose you never come for them?

HELENE: Then let it be a part payment for all you've done for us. Please. Won't you?

115   MARIE: Steve! Renard just came in. He's on his way up.

MORGAN: Did he see you?

MARIE: I don't think so.

MORGAN: All right. Now, here. You take these, and both you get in there (indicating bathroom, not bedroom) and keep quiet. Soon as I get rid of him, you take her back down to the cellar.

MARIE: All right, Steve.

116   RENARD: Good evening. May we come in?

MORGAN: Good evening. (As he's frisked.) No, I never carry 'em. What's on your mind?

RENARD: The whereabouts of the two people we are searching for.

MORGAN: Oh, you haven't found 'em yet?

RENARD: No. But since this morning through our sources we have learned their names: Monsieur and Madame de Bursac. That is correct, is it not?

MORGAN: How would I know that?

RENARD: Well, I thought, perhaps. Very nice perfume.

MORGAN: You like that, huh?

RENARD: Yes.

MORGAN: So do I. All right, Slim. Come out. You've, uh, met the boys.

MARIE: Good evening.

RENARD: Mademoiselle.

117   RENARD: Except your friend, Mr. Eddy, as he likes to be called.

MORGAN: So you got 'im.

RENARD: Yes. Now we lack only the two missing persons.

MORGAN: What are you gonna do with him?

RENARD: If you will not give us the information we want, perhaps he will. Before we made the mistake of giving him liquor; this time we will withhold it.

MORGAN: You know what that'll do to him?

RENARD: I think so.

MORGAN: He couldn't stand it. He'd crack up.

RENARD: You could easily prevent that.

MORGAN: Yeah, I can. Yuh got a cigarette? Can't you make him talk?

RENARD: When necessary.

MORGAN: You'll find some in that drawer, Slim.

RENARD: You could save Mr. Eddy a great deal of—er, shall we say, discomfort?

MARIE: Steve!

RENARD: And me a lot of time if you will tell us where these people are.

MORGAN: How much was it you were going to give me? More than what's mine already?

RENARD: I do not think now I will have to pay anybody anything.

MORGAN: You're probably right. I haven't got a match.

BODYGUARD: Don't go any—

118   MORGAN: All right, go on. Get 'em up. Go on. Go on, pull your guns. Go ahead. Go ahead. Get 'em out. Go ahead. Try it. You're gonna get it anyway.

RENARD: Harry, don't, don't—

MORGAN: You've been pushin' me around long enough. So you were gonna drive Eddy nuts. Pickin' on a poor old rummy that never— Slappin' girls around. That's right, go for it! Your boy needs company. (His gun hand shakes.) Look at that. Ain't that silly? That's how close you came. All right, Frenchy, get their guns. Here yuh are. Now get over on that couch. Go ahead, step over 'im. Sit down. All right, come on out. (Helene comes out.) That's one of 'em. The other one's down in the cellar. Frenchy, take her downstairs. Get some help. Have them both ready to leave on the boat. Then come back up here. Slim, you pack. We're shovin' off as soon as we get Eddy out.

MARIE: Okay, Steve.

RENARD: Just how do you think you—

MORGAN: Shut up! You want to know how I'm gonna get 'im out? That broke as easy as you will. There's a telephone out in the hall. You're gonna tell someone to let 'im go. Send him back up here. Oh, yes you are. One of you. I haven't forgotten you. You're both gonna take a beating till someone uses that phone. That means one of you's gonna take a beating for nothing. I don't care which one it is. I'll start with you.

119   It is Renard, not Coyo, on the phone.

RENARD: You will release him immediately.

MORGAN: Tell him you'll explain later.

RENARD: I will explain it later.

MORGAN: Tell 'im to send him back to the hotel and do nothing else till you get there.

RENARD: Send him back here to the hotel and do nothing until you hear from us.

MORGAN: All right—inside. You've got some harbor passes to fill out.

120   MORGAN: And now Paul and Madame de Bursac. I'll be right with you, Frenchy. They're all yours now.

MERCIER: Thanks, Mr. Morgan.

GERARD: They are all ready, Harry.

MORGAN: Here you are. These'll get 'em through the guard and on the boat.

GERARD: Where will you take them, Harry?

MORGAN: Well, maybe Devil's Island.

GERARD: What?

MORGAN: Might even get your friend Villemars off. That's what you wanted, wasn't it?

GERARD: Very much. Why, why are you doing this, Harry?

MORGAN (laughing): Well, I don't know. Maybe because I like you and maybe because I don't like them.

GERARD: I'm glad you are on our side, Harry. I'm glad—

MORGAN: No kissin', Frenchy.

GERARD: Oh. (Laughing.)

MORGAN: You know you'll have to take care of those guys in there.

GERARD: We will give you plenty of time!

MORGAN: If you let 'em go they'll come back here and burn this place down.

GERARD: Let them. It will be a very small fire. When Villemars comes back it will be our turn, then. We'll start a bigger one.

MORGAN: Meet you on the boat.

GUARD: One minute, please—

EDDY: Well, I—

MORGAN: That's all right. Let 'im through.

121   MORGAN: It's all right now.

EDDY: Say, you look glad to see me. You know, a funny thing—

MORGAN: Yeah, I know.

EDDY: I don't know what they wanted but they wouldn't even give me a—

MORGAN: I'll get you one down on the boat. We're leavin', Eddy. Ready, Slim?

MARIE: In a minute, Steve. Close that, will yuh?

EDDY: Say, what is this? She goin' with us?

MORGAN: Yeah, it looks like it.

EDDY: Aw, Harry, yuh mean— What's she got— Er, who are you?

122 EDDY: I feel like I was talkin' to myself.

MARIE: I bet I've been bit a hundred times that way.

EDDY: Why don't you bite 'em back?

123 EDDY: Oh. (Laughing.) I remember you. You're all right. She can come, Harry. It's okay with me. Now I'll have the two of you to take care of, won't I?

MORGAN: That's right, Eddy. You can begin by grabbin' these bags. Come on, Slim!

124 MARIE: Steve, do I have time to say good-by to Cricket?

MORGAN: Sure, go ahead.

MARIE: Cricket, I came to say good-by.

CRICKET: What?

MARIE: We're leaving now. Thanks for everything.

CRICKET: Hey, Slim. Are you still happy?

MARIE: What do you think?

Production Credits

Produced and directed by	Howard Hawks
Screenplay by	Jules Furthman
	and William Faulkner
Based on the novel by	Ernest Hemingway
Director of Photography	Sid Hickox, A.S.C.
Art Director	Charles Novi
Film Editor	Christian Nyby
Special effects by	Roy Davidson
	and Rex Wimpy, A.S.C.
Sound by	Oliver S. Garretson
Set decorations by	Casey Roberts
Technical Advisor	Louis Comien
Gowns by	Milo Anderson
Make-up Artist	Perc Westmore
"Am I Blue":	
Music by	Harry Akst
Lyrics by	Grant Drake
"Hong Kong Blues":	
Music and lyrics by	Hoagy Carmichael
"How Little We Know":	
Music by	Hoagy Carmichael
Lyrics by	Johnny Mercer
Musical Director	Leo F. Forbstein
Assistant Director	Jack Sullivan
Unit Manager	Chuck Hansen
Unit Publicist	Bill Rice

Released: October 1944
Running time: 100 minutes

Cast

Harry Morgan	Humphrey Bogart
Eddy	Walter Brennan
Marie Browning	Lauren Bacall
Helene de Bursac	Dolores Moran
Cricket	Hoagy Carmichael
Paul de Bursac	Walter Molnar
Lieutenant Coyo	Sheldon Leonard
Frenchy/Gerard	Marcel Dalio
Johnson	Walter Sande
Captain Renard	Dan Seymour
Renard's bodyguard	Aldo Nadi
Beauclerc	Paul Marion
Mrs. Beauclerc	Patricia Shay
Bartender	Pat West
Emil	Emmet Smith
Horatio	Sir Lancelot
Rosalie	Janette Grae
Quartermaster	Eugene Borden
Negro urchins	Elzie Emanuel
	Harold Garrison
Civilian	Pedro Regas
Headwaiter	Major Fred Farrell
Cashier	Adrienne d'Ambricourt
De Gaullists	Maurice Marsac
	Fred Dosch
	George Suzanne
	Louis Mercier
	Crane Whitley

Cast

Detective	Hal Kelly
Chef	Chef (Joseph) Milani
Naval Ensign	Ron Randell
Dancer	Audrey Armstrong
Cashier	Marguerite Sylva

This comprehensive cast list was compiled from the press book and from Paul Michael and others, eds., *The American Movies Reference Book* (Englewood Cliffs, N.J.: Prentice-Hall, 1969), p. 522.

Inventory

The following materials from the Warner library of the Wisconsin Center for Film and Theater Reserach were used by Kawin in preparing *To Have and Have Not* for the Wisconsin/Warner Bros. Screenplay Series:

Temporary, by Jules Furthman, October 14, 1943, with revisions to November 23, 1943, 208 pages.

Revised Temporary, by Furthman, December 30, 1943, with revisions to January 5, 1944, 111 pages, unfinished.

Final, by Furthman, January 22, 1944, with revisions to February 14, 1944, 151 pages.

Second Revised Final, by Furthman and William Faulkner, February 26, 1944, with revisions to April 22, 1944, 112 pages.

DESIGNED BY GARY GORE
COMPOSED BY GRAPHIC COMPOSITION, INC.
ATHENS, GEORGIA
MANUFACTURED BY INTER-COLLEGIATE PRESS, INC.
SHAWNEE MISSION, KANSAS
TEXT AND DISPLAY LINES ARE SET IN PALATINO

Library of Congress Cataloging in Publication Data
Furthman, Jules.
To have and have not.
(Wisconsin/Warner Bros. screenplay series)
I. Faulkner, William, 1897–1962, joint author.
II. Hemingway, Ernest, 1899–1961. To have and have not.
III. Kawin, Bruce F., 1945– IV. Title. V. Series.
PN1997.T59   791.43'7   79–5403
ISBN 0–299–08090–0
ISBN 0–299–08094–3 pbk.

WISCONSIN/WARNER BROS SCREENPLAY SERIES

The Wisconsin / Warner Bros. Screenplay Series, a product of the Warner Brothers Film Library, will enable film scholars, students, researchers, and aficionados to gain insights into individual American films in ways never before possible.

The Warner library was acquired in 1957 by the United Artists Corporation, which in turn donated it to the Wisconsin Center for Film and Theater Research in 1969. The massive library, housed in the State Historical Society of Wisconsin, contains eight hundred sound feature films, fifteen hundred short subjects, and nineteen thousand still negatives, as well as the legal files, press books, and screenplays of virtually every Warner film produced from 1930 until 1950. This rich treasure trove has made the University of Wisconsin one of the major centers for film research, attracting scholars from around the world. This series of published screenplays represents a creative use of the Warner library, both a boon to scholars and a tribute to United Artists.

Most published film scripts are literal transcriptions of finished films. The Wisconsin / Warner screenplays are primary source documents—the final shooting versions including revisions made during production. As such, they will explicate the art of screenwriting as film transcriptions cannot. They will help the user to understand the arts of directing and acting, as well as the other arts involved in the film-making process, in comparing these screenplays with the final films. (Films of the Warner library are available at modest rates from the United Artists nontheatrical rental library, United Artists/16 mm.)

From the eight hundred feature films in the library, the general editor and the editorial committee of the series have chosen those that have received critical recognition for their excellence of directing, screenwriting, and acting, films that are distinctive examples of their genre, those that have particular historical relevance, and some that are adaptations of well-known novels and plays. The researcher, instructor, or student can, in the judicious selection of individual volumes for close examination, gain a heightened appreciation and broad understanding of the American film and its historical role during this critical period.